WEIRD WAR
CURIOUS MILITARY TRIVIA

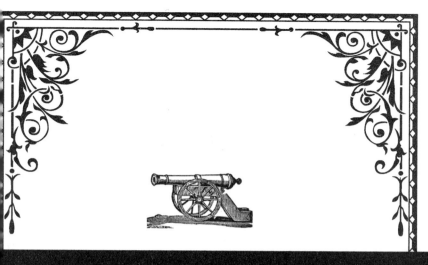

WEIRD WAR
CURIOUS MILITARY TRIVIA

ALAN AXELROD

FALL RIVER PRESS

New York

FALL RIVER PRESS

New York

An Imprint of Sterling Publishing
387 Park Avenue South
New York, NY 10016

Cover design by Scott Russo
Book design by Kevin Ullrich

ISBN 978-1-4351-4423-1 (print format)
ISBN 978-1-4351-4485-9 (ebook)

Distributed in Canada by Sterling Publishing
^{C}/o Canadian Manda Group, 165 Dufferin Street
Toronto, Ontario, Canada M6K 3H6
Distributed in the United Kingdom by GMC Distribution Services
Castle Place, 166 High Street, Lewes, East Sussex, England BN7 1XU
Distributed in Australia by Capricorn Link (Australia) Pty. Ltd.
P.O. Box 704, Windsor, NSW 2756, Australia

For information about custom editions, special sales, and premium and corporate purchases, please contact Sterling Special Sales at 800-805-5489 or specialsales@sterlingpublishing.com.

Manufactured in the United States of America
2 4 6 8 10 9 7 5 3 1
www.sterlingpublishing.com

For Anita and Ian

Contents

Introduction

A History of Violence

Modern historians have estimated that from 3,500 or so years of recorded "civilization" there is to be eked out a mere 230 years of peace—that is, periods in which no war was being fought by some group somewhere over something. We may like to think of history as the story of life in particular places and periods, but it is just as accurate to call it a story of violence.

Except perhaps for sex, nothing has generated more cultural, pop cultural, and creative interest than war. From such literary works as the *Epic of Gilgamesh*, Homer's *Iliad*, *War and Peace*, and *The Naked and the Dead*, to such movies as *The Birth of a Nation* and *Saving Private Ryan*, authors and filmmakers have celebrated, even as historians have chronicled, the exploits of a band of warriors or a vast army of professional soldiers bent on shaping or reshaping their patch of earth, if not the entire world, through a clash of arms.

Again, except perhaps for sex, nothing has created more titillating, fascinating, and appalling curiosities of fact, trivia, and just plain weirdness than war. From Sun Tzu to Herodotus to Carl von Clausewitz to John Keegan, historians and military theorists have grappled with the essential nature and conduct of war, without arriving at an analysis sufficiently broad to cover all its philosophical, psychological, technological, and legal implications. In this book, I don't even try. I just revel in the random, revelatory weirdness of it all, and I invite readers to revel with me.

It is, to be sure, a guilty pleasure. Yet the fact is that the vocation of armies and navies and air forces is to kill people and break things, and such activities involve extremes of thought, passion, horror, sacrifice, and commitment. Outlandish customs, bizarre rules, unusual personalities, once-in-a-lifetime events, and strange behavior are all bound to be churned up and churned out in florid abundance.

"In the midst of life we are in death," says the *Book of Common Prayer*. War—the bringer of death itself—turns this sentence on its head: *In the midst of death, we are in life.* As British general Sir Ian Hamilton wrote in his diary during the Battle of Gallipoli, among the most tragic and futile battles in what may have been the most tragic and futile of modern wars, "There are poets and writers who see naught in war but carrion, filth, savagery, and horror. . . . The superb moral victory over death leaves them cold. Each one to his taste. To me this is no valley of death—it is a valley brim full of life at its highest power." And life, raised to the apex of intensity because it is lived at the edge of death, cannot but yield facts, follies, and figures so strange, so remarkable, so vivid as to be well worth their collection and contemplation. For this reason and for no other: reader, forward, march!

"It is well that war is so terrible—we would grow too fond of it."

—General Robert E. Lee to Lieutenant General James Longstreet,
surveying the carnage at the Battle of Fredericksburg, December 13, 1862

"Four things greater than all things are—
Women and Horses and Power and War."

—Rudyard Kipling, "The Ballad of the King's Jest," 1890

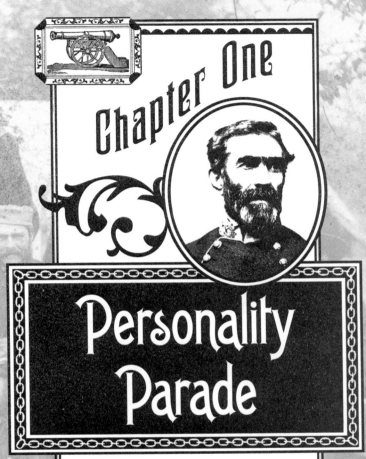

Chapter One

Personality Parade

FACTS ABOUT CIVILIANS AND SOLDIERS— THE GOOD, THE BAD, AND THE LUCKY

Subject to Dispute

A product of the West Point class of 1837, Braxton Bragg (1817–1876) fought for the Confederacy during the Civil War (1861–1865). He exhibited flashes of brilliance, as when, after the Battle of Shiloh, he put his entire army on a train to ride the long way round to Chattanooga, where he managed to checkmate Union general Don Carlos Buell. Mostly, however, Bragg showed himself to be unimaginative, indecisive, hesitant, insufficiently aggressive, unwilling to exploit his few victories, generally contemptuous of others, and pathologically disputatious—in short, a real charmer.

To say he was unpopular with his men would be an understatement. During the U.S.-Mexican War (1846–1848), he was twice the intended target of what today would be called "fragging": assassination by those under his command. One attempt involved the detonation of a twelve-pound explosive artillery shell under the cot he slept on. The cot was a total loss. Bragg escaped without a scratch.

He argued, constantly and with everybody. In his post–Civil War *Private Memoirs*, Ulysses S. Grant recorded an anecdote he called "very characteristic of Bragg." During the early 1840s, Bragg was assigned to a far western fort, which, like all remote army outposts of the era, was severely undermanned. Bragg was therefore obliged to serve both as a company commander and as the post quartermaster, the officer in charge of supplies. Grant related that Bragg, as company commander, once submitted to the quartermaster—who was also himself—a requisition for company supplies. As quartermaster, however, Bragg rejected Bragg's own request. Undaunted, in his capacity as company commander, Bragg resubmitted the

Opposite: Braxton Bragg in the uniform of a Confederate general.

document, revised to include an elaborate justification for the expense. Once again, however, as quartermaster, Bragg rejected it.

Seeing no means of resolution, Braxton Bragg appealed to the post commandant, who sputtered: "My God, Mr. Bragg, you have quarreled with every officer in the army, and now you are quarreling with yourself!"

The Rebel Rose

In the early months of the Civil War, Washington, D.C.—the capital of the Union, but in every outward characteristic a typically Southern city—was crawling with Confederate spies. One of the most alluring of them was Maryland-born Rose O'Neal Greenhow, who, after the death in 1854 of her husband, Department of State official Dr. Robert Greenhow, became the toast of Washington as a kind of merry widow. In the years leading up to the war, she was an outspoken Southern sympathizer even as she ingratiated herself with any number of influential Washington men in the government and military. When the war began, rebel spymaster Thomas Jordan recruited her as an instrument of espionage. Describing herself as "a Southern woman, born with revolutionary blood in my veins," she eagerly volunteered.

Rose set about her new profession avidly. She obtained a fair amount of information about Union plans for the First Battle of Bull Run (July 21, 1861), which she transmitted via a female courier, Betty Duvall, another comely Washingtonian who hid Greenhow's enciphered messages in what Confederate general M.L. Bonham described as "the longest and most beautiful roll of hair I have ever seen." Thanks at least in some part to Greenhow's intelligence, Confederate general Pierre Gustave Toutant Beauregard was able to deploy his forces advantageously behind

Bull Run Creek, a tactic that helped position him for a decisive and humiliating victory against Union general Irvin McDowell.

The espionage career of Rose O'Neal Greenhow, whom the tabloids of the era would soon dub "The Rebel Rose," was cut short by iconic private eye Allan Pinkerton, who shadowed her, doggedly peeped through her windows, and finally, on August 23, 1861, ran her to ground. She was held under house arrest and then consigned with her young daughter to the Old Capitol Prison, which had been built after the War of 1812 as temporary quarters for Congress until the original Capitol, burned by the British, was rebuilt. She was ultimately paroled to the South, to which she returned to a heroine's welcome. At length restless for more patriotic excitement, however, she sailed to Europe on a mission to generate support and cash for the Confederate cause. No less a figure than Emperor Napoleon III of France received her, as did Britain's Queen Victoria. Greenhow even found time to pen a memoir, *My Imprisonment and the First Year of Abolition Rule at Washington*, which sold very well abroad, raising ready cash for the Confederacy.

In August 1864, Rose boarded the British blockade-runner *Condor*, out of Greenock, Scotland, bound for the American South. The night before *Condor* entered Cape Fear River with the object of putting in at Wilmington, North Carolina, another blockade-runner, *Night Hawk*, had run aground at the mouth of the river. It was boarded by Union sailors, who set it ablaze. *Condor's* skipper, the distinguished Admiral Charles Hobart-Hampden, eighth Earl of Buckinghamshire, had entrusted the helm to a local pilot, who, as he brought the ship into the river through heavy seas, steered sharply to avoid the looming, smoldering hulk of *Night Hawk*. In so doing, however, he ran *Condor* aground on New Inlet Bar, just two hundred yards from Confederate Fort Fisher. *The London Daily Mail* subsequently carried the story:

At 3 in the morning of [September] 1st...the *Condor* [ran] aground in the breakers. . . . After the *Condor* took the ground, a Yankee vessel was seen approaching through the gloom, with a view to shelling the stranger. Mrs. Greenhow, remembering her long former imprisonment in Washington, and apprehensive of its repetition, insisted, against the advice of the captain, upon having a boat lowered, upon trusting herself to the tender mercies of the waves rather than to those of the Yankees. Into this boat she carried with her the mail bags [presumably containing secret dispatches]. . . . To the pilot, who had just run the *Condor* aground, was committed the delicate task of steering Mrs. Greenhow's boat, which was lowered into a raging surf. Directly the boat left the leeside of the vessel she was caught, broadside on, by a huge breaker, and overturned. All the male passengers succeeded in clambering up and clutching the keel of the capsized boat, but in the darkness and amid the deafening thunder of the breakers, nothing was seen or heard of poor Mrs. Greenhow. Her body was subsequently washed ashore near Fort Fisher, and close beside it a heavy leather reticule, containing $2,000 [actually, $3,000] in gold, which was believed to have been slung around her neck when the boat was upset. It is a strange proof of the strength of that boisterous sea that such a weighty article as this reticule should not have sunk, but should have been tossed up on the

Opposite: Rose O'Neal Greenhow—the "Rebel Rose."

beach like a bit of seaweed. Upon the afternoon of the 2nd
Mrs. Greenhow's body was committed to the grave at Wilmington, according to the rites of the Roman Catholic Church.

The part about the "reticule" of gold having been found beside Rose O'Neal Greenhow's body leaves out an important detail. The corpse and bag were initially discovered by a Confederate soldier, who snatched the gold and pushed the body back into the waves. Later in the day, the body washed back ashore. When it was subsequently identified as that of the "Rebel Rose," the soldier who had purloined the treasure was so affected by his conscience that he voluntarily surrendered his prize, which, presumably, was put to some good use in the service of the Confederate States of America.

I Spy

William Alvin Lloyd made a very good living publishing steamboat and railroad guides. Although he was a Northerner by birth and residence, he had the market pretty well cornered on *Southern* guidebooks—and that, of course, was a big problem when the Civil War broke out, because he was barred from crossing below the Mason-Dixon Line.

Desperate to salvage his livelihood, Lloyd called on President Abraham Lincoln during the summer of 1861 to ask for an executive passport that would allow him to travel and trade in the Confederate States of America. His request wasn't as extraordinary as it sounds. Throughout the Civil War—and especially early in the conflict—both Presidents Lincoln and Davis routinely issued passes to permit some travel and trade. Nevertheless, Lincoln was not about to give Lloyd what he wanted, at least not for free. He told Lloyd that he could indeed have the passport, provided that he agreed to serve as his personal spy, reporting directly and only to him.

At first, the quiet publisher had absolutely no interest in risking his neck, but, envisioning the imminent demise of his business, he rapidly rethought his priorities and accepted passports, not only for himself, but also for his business associates Thomas H.S. Boyd and F. J. Bonfanti as well as his own wife and her chambermaid. The president personally drew up a contract, which stipulated that Lloyd would record the number of Confederate troops he found at specified points, that he would obtain the plans of Confederate forts, that he would not use any codes or ciphers, and that he would report directly and exclusively to the president. Best of all, he would receive $200 a month plus expenses.

Lloyd proved to be a diligent and resourceful spy, and over the full four years of the war he remained in the South, sending Lincoln maps of fortifications and harbors as well as reports on troop strength. The president, it is believed, used these to check on the accuracy of reports his own generals submitted to him. That Lloyd was able to supply any intelligence at all is astounding. For one thing, because he was forbidden to use code or to send messages via the Union army (he was to report to the president and the president alone), he had to send telegrams to family members living in Washington, who then passed the dispatches to the president— but usually after very considerable delay, as these telegrams were first passed around the family for their entertainment. Also, Lloyd was none too subtle about his spying, and he frequently aroused suspicion. He was repeatedly detained by Confederate authorities for questioning and was even jailed four times, perhaps even more. On one occasion, the sixty-one-year-old provost marshal of Richmond (and commanding officer of Confederate POW camps), General John H. Winder, summoned Lloyd to a personal interview. Lloyd responded by buying the general expensive groceries and ordering for him a resplendent bespoke dress uniform for the spectacular sum of $1,200 (U.S.): the equivalent of more than $27,000 in today's money. Winder was duly mollified.

Lloyd had his closest call on November 8, 1862, when Confederate detectives raided his house in Lynchburg, Tennessee. Worried that the only claim he had on the salary Lincoln promised him was the contract he and the president had signed, Lloyd at first kept the document neatly folded in the hat he wore at all times. At some point, it occurred to him that carrying on his person the document that certified he was not only a Union spy, but also a personal spy to the president of the United States, was not a very good idea. He therefore gave the contract to his wife for safekeeping. She, in turn, had her maid sew it into one of her dresses. Now, as the Confederate detectives ransacked the house in search of incriminating papers, Mrs. Boyd and her maid found themselves left alone together in a room. Mrs. Boyd took the opportunity to pull the contract out of her dress and then, in a frenzy of fear, tore it up into little tiny pieces, which she let fall on the floor. Suddenly realizing that the detectives would probably be suspicious when they saw a torn-up document in the middle of an otherwise spotless floor, she gathered the pieces and tossed them into the fireplace—thereby destroying the only evidence her husband had of his official employment.

Although the family was saved from incarceration or even execution, Lloyd, at the conclusion of the war, pleaded in vain for his unpaid salary, which amounted to $9,753.32, by his meticulous calculation. He was able to recite the contents of the destroyed contract by heart, but the only man who could corroborate these terms, Abraham Lincoln, had been murdered on April 14, 1865, by John Wilkes Booth. Congress eventually reimbursed the Lloyds for documented expenses to the tune of

$2,380, but refused to pay the salary demanded. Lloyd died in 1868, and seven years later, in 1875, Enoch Totten, the attorney administering his estate, sued the United States for payment. The suit was rejected on the grounds that the six-year statute of limitations for such claims had expired. Totten then appealed to the Supreme Court, which upheld the lower court's decision. The salary was never paid.

3,468 to 1

As of 2012, 3,469 Medals of Honor—the nation's highest military medal—have been awarded: 3,468 to men, and 1 to a woman. And that single medal, having been awarded, was subsequently "deleted," but ultimately restored.

Born in 1832 in Oswego, New York, Mary Edwards Walker graduated from Syracuse Medical College (today Upstate Medical University) in 1855, the only woman in her class. She set up a joint practice with her husband, Albert Miller, in Rome, New York, but few people wanted to be treated by a "lady" doctor, and the practice went bust. With the outbreak of the Civil War, Walker volunteered her professional services. She was accepted—but, at first, only as a nurse. At last, in September 1863, the Army of the Cumberland hired her as a "Contract Assisting Surgeon (civilian)," making her the first female surgeon to be employed by the U.S. Army. Subsequently appointed assistant surgeon of the Fifty-Second Ohio Infantry, she was captured by Confederates just south of the Georgia-Tennessee border on April 10, 1864, and accused of being a spy. She may well have been one, although, at the time of her capture, she had just finished aiding a Confederate surgeon in performing an amputation.

Imprisoned in Richmond, Virginia, for just over four months, Dr. Walker was released in a prisoner exchange, and she resumed serving as a Union army surgeon and, perhaps, even as a spy. After the war, Walker lectured and wrote on health care, temperance, women's rights, and—most controversial in her day—the subject of "dress reform." She advocated that women should wear male attire, which she considered more practical than traditional female clothing, and she was several times even arrested on charges of "impersonating a man."

Immediately after the Civil War, Generals William Tecumseh Sherman and George Henry "Rock of Chickamauga" Thomas jointly recommended Dr. Walker for a Medal of Honor. On November 11, 1865, President Andrew Johnson signed a bill to present her with the medal, which was duly awarded. The woman wore it proudly every day thereafter.

In the so-called "Purge of 1917," the U.S. Army reviewed the Medal of Honor roll and rescinded—the army's term was "deleted"—awards its leadership now considered undeserved. These included Medals of Honor given to officers and men of the 27th Maine simply as incentives to reenlistment and to the twenty-nine troops who accompanied Lincoln's body from Washington to Springfield, Illinois. Among the 911 recipients "deleted" in the purge were Buffalo Bill Cody and Mary Walker, neither of whom was an officially enlisted member of the army. Walker declared that the army could have her medal back "over my dead body"—but, in fact, the army never requested the return of any of the medals it had "deleted," and it also declined to "police" the wearing of them. As for Walker, she wore the honor to her grave. She died in 1919, two years after the deletion, at the age of eighty-six. In 1977, President Jimmy Carter issued an executive order posthumously restoring her Medal of Honor.

Opposite: Dr. Mary Edwards Walker is the only woman to be awarded the Medal of Honor (so far).

The Glorious Amputee

José Millán-Astray (1879–1954) founded the Spanish Foreign Legion in 1920, made up a no-nonsense motto for it—*Viva la muerte!* ("Long live death!")—then led it against rebellious Northern Moroccan Berber tribesmen in the Rif War of 1920–1926. Here he lost (in order of disappearance) his left arm, his right eye, and assorted fingers from his right hand. He was dubbed henceforth "El Glorioso mutilado," which may be translated as the "Glorious Amputee" or, more literally, the "Glorious Mutilated One."

Leaving about 20 percent of himself in Morocco may not actually have been the worst thing to happen to Millán-Astray. Fourteen years earlier, in 1906, he had married a general's daughter, the lovely Elvira Gutiérrez de la Torre. What could possibly be wrong with that? Having made what he and everyone else deemed a spectacular career-advancing connection to an attractive woman, the wedding was a joyous occasion.

The wedding night? Not so much.

Shortly after entering the bridal chamber, Elvira proclaimed to her groom that she intended to "remain chaste" henceforth. And so began what the Glorious Amputee described as a "fraternal relationship." This lasted until 1941, when he fell in love with one Rita Gasset during what was apparently a very hot game of contract bridge. Although Millán-Astray separated from the fraternal Elvira, he never did marry Rita, even after the two produced a daughter, Peregrina, his only child.

Above: General José Millán-Astray, founder of the Spanish Foreign Legion, leaves the headquarters of Fascist leader General Francisco Franco. Note the missing right eye, empty left sleeve, and mutilated right hand.

The Eater of Men, the Pooper, and the Unprepared

A good military nickname can be an asset to any commander. Alexander was "The Great," the Civil War's General George H. Thomas was "The Rock of Chickamauga," John J. Pershing of World War I fame was "Black Jack," George S. Patton Jr. was "Old Blood and Guts," and H. Norman Schwarzkopf copped "Stormin' Norman." The list goes on.

One of the most fearsome of all *noms de guerre* was bestowed upon General Charles Emmanuel Marie Mangin (1866–1925), commander, successively, of the French Third, Sixth, and Tenth Armies, and a combatant in the World War I battles of Verdun, the Aisne, and Second Marne. He earned his nickname, "The Eater of

General George H. Thomas
"The Rock of Chickamauga"

General John J. Pershing
"Black Jack"

Men"—sometimes simplified to "The Butcher"—less for what he did to the enemy than for his unbounded and unconditional faith in what the French liked to call *la guerre à outrance*, "war to the extreme." For him, the command was always *attack*, *attack*, and again *attack*. Personally immune to fear, he was also more than willing to spend the lives of his men, many of whom cordially hated him for it.

His response? "Whatever you do, you lose a lot of men."

And that he did.

Mangin's moniker was invented by his men, while that of Constantine V (718–775) came from his enemies. It would be hard to tell him apart from the bewildering slew of Byzantine warrior emperors who preceded and followed him, were it not for those foes who bestowed upon him a nickname destined to live in infamy: *Kopronymos*. Now, if you don't know Greek, this may not sound too bad, but

General George S. Patton Jr.
"Old Blood and Guts"

General H. Norman Schwarzkopf
"Stormin' Norman"

when you parse it out in English, you discover that it means "Dung-Named," and so he was Constantine the Dung-Named.

This was no idle instance of trash talking. The nasty handle commemorates a little stunt he pulled in infancy during his own baptism when he took an unceremonious and malodorous dump in the baptismal font. Worse, evidently no one who saw—or smelled—it ever forgot or forgave it.

But maybe neither Man Eater nor Dung-Named is quite so objectionable a name-branding as what befell the man who reigned as a Dark Age king of England from 978 to 1016. Ethelred II—or, if you insist on a ligature, Æthelred II—was a Saxon ruler who got a lot of bad advice and so became known to history as Ethelred Unraed, *unraed* being the Old English word for "bad counsel." That was a crappy enough nickname, to be sure, but it got even worse. Universally mistranslated into modern English, *unraed* came out as "unready" and therefore a monarch who was actually one of the fiercest and most forceful warrior kings of England's pre–Norman Conquest era became known to posterity as Ethelred the Unready.

The Coventry Blitz Myth

Coventry, a city of a quarter-million people in the industrial West Midlands of England, was a frequent target of German air raids during World War II. The most catastrophic of these attacks, the "Coventry Blitz," came on November 14, 1940, when 515 bombers hit the city. The raid destroyed 4,000 homes, damaged two-thirds of all buildings, damaged or destroyed a third of the city's factories, and reduced the fourteenth-century Gothic masterpiece, Coventry Cathedral, to a gutted shell. An estimated 568 persons were killed and 1,256 injured in the air raid.

Beginning in the 1970s, a series of authors churned out books and articles claiming that Coventry had been the victim not merely of German bombs, but of Prime Minister Winston Churchill's decision to sacrifice the city, its cathedral, and its people rather than compromise what he (and others) considered a war-winning source of intelligence: the fact that British code breakers had what they called "Ultra," the key to Germany's supposedly impregnable "Enigma" cypher.

Above: A lone figure surveys the ruin of Coventry Cathedral, November, 1940.

In 1974's *The Ultra Secret*, former RAF Group Captain F. W. Winterbotham not only revealed for the first time that the Allies had broken Enigma but also claimed that the word "Coventry" had been intercepted and decrypted by three o'clock on the afternoon of November 14—mere hours before the late-night raid. Winterbotham claimed to have personally telephoned the information to one of Churchill's Downing Street secretaries. Other authors, Anthony Cave Brown (*Bodyguard of Lies*, 1974) and William Stevenson (*A Man Called Intrepid*, 1976), told similar stories, albeit with critical differences in the details—including the claim by Cave Brown that Churchill had a full *forty-eight hours'* advance warning, not just same-day intelligence.

Whereas those who have disseminated the story—that Churchill chose to ignore the intercept rather than warn Coventry (and thereby betray to Berlin Britain's knowledge of Enigma)—point to the similarities in the three 1970s accounts for proof of the tale's truth, it is the differences that cast persuasive doubt on them. In fact, *The Wizard War*, written in 1978 by Dr. R. V. Jones, one of the British Air Ministry's top scientists, convincingly explains that the messages that were actually intercepted and decrypted persuaded everyone that the target of the November 14–15 raid would certainly be London, along with three or four other targets in the south of England—not the northerly West Midlands. This assumption was corroborated by a captured German map, on which only southern target areas were marked. On November 12, according to Jones, a decrypt was received that did indicate a raid on Coventry, but it did not appear to be connected with the imminent raids apparently planned against London and other southern targets. Jones specifically denies that anyone at Downing Street received a phone call from Winterbotham.

Another authoritative figure, John Colville, one of Churchill's private secretaries, confirmed in his 1981 memoir, *The Churchillians*, that no one connected with Enigma decrypts wanted to arouse "German suspicions . . . for the sake of ephemeral advantages." But, he added, as for Coventry, "until the German [radio-homing] directional beam"—which the British had learned to track covertly—"was turned on the doomed city, nobody knew where the great raid would be. Certainly the Prime Minister did not."

Colville recorded in his diary at the time that "obviously some major [German] air operation [was coming], but its exact destination the Air Ministry find it difficult to determine." As for Churchill himself, assuming that the main raid would in fact be against London, he altered his routine of spending a few days in Oxfordshire and instead resolved to remain in London. It was always important to him that he share all dangers with his fellow Londoners. Ordering the female Downing Street staff to go home before dark, he himself, on the night of November 14–15, ascended to the roof of the Air Ministry to "watch the fireworks."

They did not come, not to London that night. That night, it was Coventry that burned.

☆ ☆ ☆

"I'm sorry. All five."

The oldest, George Thomas Sullivan, was twenty-seven, the youngest, Albert "Al"
Leo Sullivan, twenty. The other three Sullivan brothers—Francis "Frank,"
Joseph "Joe," and Madison "Matt"—were twenty-six, twenty-four, and twenty-
three. Born and raised in Waterloo, Iowa, they all joined the navy on January 3,
1942, little more than three weeks after Pearl Harbor. Patriotic though they were,
they had one condition. They told the recruiter that, if they joined, they had to be
allowed to serve together, on the same ship. Technically, this presented a problem,
since the U.S. Navy had a policy of separating brothers, hoping to keep any one
family's loss as minimal as possible. But the regulation was loosely enforced at
best, and the idea of the five "boys" doing "their bit" together was universally
appealing. Navy brass agreed, and the Sullivans were enlisted.

Their ship, the light cruiser *Juneau*, was fighting off Guadalcanal on the morning of November 13, 1942, when it was hit by a Japanese torpedo. Badly damaged, it
had to limp away. That same day, while convoying with other wounded vessels to a
rear-area base at Espiritu Santo, *Juneau* was hit again. This time the enemy torpedo
struck its powder magazines. *Juneau* exploded and quickly went to the bottom.

It was a loss so obviously catastrophic that the convoy's senior officer, the
skipper of the cruiser *Helena*, made the hard call to avoid lingering to look for

Above: The Sullivan brothers on board the USS *Juneau*, from left to right: Joseph, Francis, Albert, Madison, and George.

the five Sullivan brothers
"missing in action" off the Solomons

THEY DID THEIR PART

survivors. He knew the Japanese sub was still lurking, and every ship in the convoy was as vulnerable as *Juneau* had been.

The tragic fact was that nearly a hundred *Juneau* crewmembers had survived the blast and the sinking. Although a B-17 saw them in the water, the pilot was under the same strict radio-silence orders that applied to *Helena*. He was forbidden to report the sighting until he landed hours later. By the time anyone actually went looking for the sailors, days had passed, and only ten men were recovered alive. The rest had succumbed to exposure, hunger, thirst, injury, and sharks. There were lots of sharks.

In final scene of *The Fighting Sullivans*, a 1944 Hollywood movie about the brothers, when *Juneau* is hit, the screen just goes black. The implication is that the young men died instantly and died as they had served—together. In fact, the ten rescued sailors reported that Frank, Joe, and Matt had indeed gone down with the ship, but Al drowned a day after the sinking, and George clung to life for four or maybe five days, before becoming increasingly delirious from exposure to the elements and from swallowing or deliberately drinking seawater. Crazed, he jumped over the side of the raft. Some attributed this not to consumption of saltwater, but to mad grief for the loss of the other four Sullivans.

Tight wartime security delayed notification of the brothers' parents until January 12, 1943. On that day, three men in Class A navy uniforms called at the house in Waterloo.

"I have some news for you about your boys," the senior among them announced.

"Which one?" father Thomas Sullivan grimly asked.

"I'm sorry. All five."

Chesty

Like many U.S. Marines, Lewis Burwell Puller (1898–1971) was a big man. His broad barrel chest might have been sufficient in itself to have earned him the nickname by which he became a fixture of USMC lore: "Chesty." What sealed the deal, however, was the profusion of ribbons and medals that eventually adorned that chest, which, massive though it was, could hardly hold them all. There were twenty-seven different decorations (some awarded in multiples) arrayed in seven rows: the Navy Cross with four award stars; Distinguished Service Cross; Silver Star; Legion of Merit with one award star and valor device; Bronze Star with valor device; Purple Heart; Air Medal with two award stars; Navy Presidential Unit Citation with five service stars; Marine Corps Good Conduct Medal with one service star; Marine Corps Expeditionary Medal with one service star; World War I Victory Medal with West Indies clasp; Haitian Campaign Medal, 1921; Nicaraguan Campaign Medal, 1933; China Service Medal; American Defense Service Medal with Base clasps; American Campaign Medal; Asiatic-Pacific Campaign Medal with four service stars; World War II Victory Medal; National Defense Service Medal; Korean Service Medal with five service stars; Haitian *Medaille Militaire*; Nicaraguan Presidential Medal of Merit (with Diploma); Nicaraguan Cross of Valor (with Diploma); Order of Military Merit, Eulji Cordon Medal; Chinese Order of the Sword and Banner; Korean Presidential Unit Citation; and the United Nations Korea Medal. "Chesty" was the most highly decorated Marine in the history of the Corps.

Opposite: Among his many decorations, General Lewis Burwell "Chesty" Puller received the Navy Cross for *five* separate actions.

A Mother's Love

Paul Tibbets, Jr., was a colonel in the U.S. Army Air Forces when he was given the assignment of dropping the world's first operational atomic bomb on Japan. Born in Quincy, Illinois, he had grown up in Cedar Rapids, Iowa, the son of a candy wholesaler. Judging from the name he painted on the fuselage of his B-29, serial number 44-86292, however, it was not his father who made the deepest impression on him. Tibbets named his bomber after his mother: "Enola Gay." The bomb that Tibbets dropped on Hiroshima, on August 6, 1945, killed 80,000 people instantly and possibly tens of thousands more over the following months. Mrs. Tibbets considered her son a hero. Whether or not she appreciated her name being connected with so lethal an event, however, is not known.

America's Most Famous Soldier

In January 1956, Elvis Presley made his first big-time RCA album, and his phenomenal pop-culture breakout began. That year as well, having turned twenty-one, Elvis was also eligible for the military draft.

The singer's crafty—many would say ruthless—agent/manager, Colonel Tom Parker, wrote to the Pentagon to ask that his client be considered for a Special Services assignment, which would make him essentially an entertainer in uniform. Yet Parker also realized that Elvis's performances for the U.S. Army would become the property of the U.S. government. Singing for free, Parker believed, would damage "his" property. Telling Elvis that a cushy Special Services slot was a bad business move, he assured his client that he could finagle avoidance of the draft altogether. Yet, even as he floated this reassuring prospect, Parker began to realize that

military service would actually do the Elvis Presley brand a lot of good. It would counter the negative publicity already being generated by his client's sexually charged performances. Focusing on his gyrating hips, reporters had dubbed him "Elvis the Pelvis," and many a parent was up in arms. Parker did not want to obliterate Elvis's bad-boy image, but he also did not want to alienate the families of his teenage audience or to foreclose the possibility of winning over a more mature audience in addition to the youthful horde.

So Parker finally broke it to Elvis this way: The chance to serve in what was, in the late 1950s, a peacetime army was a golden opportunity—but only if he served as a "regular" soldier. Put in your required two years, Parker promised his client, and you will return an even bigger star than you are now.

Elvis Presley pushed back—hard—but finally gave in, reporting for a pre-induction physical on January 4, 1957. A little less than a year later, he was notified that his induction was imminent. The U.S. Navy tried to preempt the army by offering to create an "Elvis Presley Company," to arrange Las Vegas performing dates for him and the company, and to lodge him in private quarters. The army responded

Opposite: Newly inducted Private Elvis Presley laces on his combat boots for the first time.

by dangling a fabulous world tour and enlistment in Special Services—minus the discomforts and inconvenience of Basic Training.

Parker advised that accepting either of these sweetheart deals would turn America against Elvis. He did, however, negotiate a draft deferment to allow his client to film *King Creole*. The American public's angry response to the extension, which it condemned as "special treatment," vindicated Parker's approach to the entire question of military service. The people were pissed.

Elvis's legion of fans called March 24, 1958, the day of his induction, "Black Monday." Parker ensured that the entire process was well covered by the press. But, after that, the young man who was now America's most famous GI and who had hated the very idea of serving, actually dedicated himself to the mission of becoming a very good soldier. As a member of the Second Armored Division's Tank Battalion, he quickly distinguished himself as a pistol marksman during training at Fort Hood. He then shipped out to West Germany with the Third Armored Division. Shortly after his arrival there, he turned down yet another offer to join Special Services, and he was assigned instead to serve as a driver, first for his company captain and then for a senior NCO.

Elvis's fellow soldiers liked him. They appreciated and admired his efforts to be seen as—and to actually be—a regular, ordinary GI. It didn't hurt any, either, that he bought television sets for his entire base. Weeks before he left Germany to return to the United States in March 1960, Elvis Presley, who had already risen from private to corporal, was promoted to sergeant. On March 5, he was honorably discharged. And Parker was proved right. When Elvis came marching home, he was bigger than ever.

Opposite: Elvis Presley was promoted to sergeant at his army unit's maneuver headquarters in Grafenwoehr, Germany, on February 11, 1960. He served with the Third Armored Division.

Chapter Two

From the Rank ~and~File Files

A GRUNT'S-EYE VIEW
OF MILITARY HISTORY

Stomach for the Fight

Napoleon famously observed that an "army travels on its stomach," and he always insisted that his soldiers be well fed so that they would fight, fight fiercely, and fight loyally. Despite this wisdom, soldiers have grumbled about their miserable rations before and since. Almost certainly, the worst food was served to the celebrated Spartans—the most feared and fearsome fighters of the ancient world. Their staple ration was called "black broth" and consisted of pork, salt, and vinegar—with a generous base of animal blood. Spartan leaders believed this bestial concoction made men into fighting animals. Sparta's enemies claimed that it only made them that much more willing to die, since only the truly crazy would consent to live long on such a diet.

☆ ☆ ☆

Why We Fight

Historians, ordinary folk, and military personnel alike have often wondered what motivates men—and women—to put themselves in harm's way. Is it patriotism? Defense of the homeland? Love of adventure? Hunger for glory? The question has often been asked, but never definitively answered—except by at least some nineteenth-century sailors in the British and American navies. They said they sailed to earn their heavenly reward.

It was a reserved patch in a kind of paradise, a realm that welcomed even the lowliest swabby into its warm embrace. Verdant and sunny, it was a place of merrymaking everlasting, where sailors and sweethearts danced to fiddle tunes for all eternity.

Called "Fiddler's Green," the earliest printed mention dates back to a sailor's tale from 1832, and says that it can be found "nine miles beyond the dwelling of his Satanic majesty." Some called it Lubber Land—a *lubber* being an inexperienced sailor—but the more inviting *Fiddler's Green* is the name that stuck, and, to this day, a slew of U.S. Navy petty officers' clubs and bars are named after it.

Most incredibly, despite the spirit of interservice rivalry that has always marked the history of the United States military, personnel of the U.S. Army and the U.S. Marine Corps freely borrowed the Fiddler's Green concept from the navy. A 1923 edition of the *Cavalry Journal* published a collection called "Fiddler's Green and other Cavalry Songs by JHS." It mentioned a campfire tale told by one Captain "Sammy" Pearson, who was posted in the Medicine Bow Mountains of Wyoming. For him and his men, "Fiddler's Green" was the idyllic destination of deceased cavalry troopers. The soldiers of modern U.S. Army units descended from the old cavalry still speak of their dead as having "passed on to Fiddler's Green."

It Wasn't Always "Always Faithful"

Everybody knows that the motto of the United States Marine Corps is *Semper Fidelis*: "Always faithful." But it wasn't always. The *current* motto was adopted in 1883. The *original* motto may have been the single Latin word *Fortitudine*, which means "With courage" or "With fortitude."

We know that *Fortitudine* predates the War of 1812 and was officially in use until 1883, but the USMC also liked *Per Mare, Per Terram*—"By Sea, By Land"—which it borrowed from the British Royal Marines, the very force it had sometimes fought.

The lamest of the pre–Semper Fi mottos may have been "To the Shores of Tripoli." A reference to the 1805 Battle of Derne against the Barbary Pirates in Tripoli during the First Barbary War of 1801–1805, it disappeared entirely in 1843, five years before the marines fought in "the Halls of Montezuma" during the Battle of Chapultepec at the conclusion of the U.S.-Mexican War of 1846–1848. Were it not for the beginning of *The Marines' Hymn*—"From the Halls of Montezuma,/To the shores of Tripoli"—both lines would probably have faded from Marine Corps public lore.

Not that *The Marines' Hymn* is entirely original. The lyrics to that celebrated service anthem came from a book of poems compiled by one W. E. Christian, published in 1917, and titled *Rhymes of the Rookies*—though it is believed that the verses actually date from the nineteenth century. The tune can be dated very precisely. It is from an 1867 revision of an 1859 opera, *Geneviève de Brabant* by Jacques Offenbach, the Parisian composer who gave the world the Can-Can.

Opposite: U.S. Marine Corps recruiting poster from the Civil War.

PRIZE MONEY! PRIZE MONEY!

RESPOND TO YOUR COUNTRY'S CALL!

Wanted for the U. S. Marine Corps
ABLE-BODIED, SOBER, INTELLIGENT MEN,

Between the ages of 18 and 40 years, not less than five feet four and a half inches high, and of good character.

Soldiers serving in this Corps perform duty at Navy Yards, and on board Vessels of War on Foreign Stations. Term of service, four years. Minors will be enlisted with the consent of their Parents or Guardians.

	PAY PER MONTH.		PAY PER YEAR.		PAY FOR 4 YEARS.
ORDERLY SERGEANT,	-	$20	-	$240	-	$960
SERGEANTS,	-	17	-	204	-	816
CORPORALS,	-	13	-	156	-	624
MUSICIANS,	-	12	-	144	-	576
PRIVATES,	-	13	-	156	-	624

In addition to the above pay, each Soldier receives $1.50 per month whilst serving on board Ships, and an ample supply of Clothing, from which he can save from $60 to $75 during his enlistment, besides medical attendance during sickness, and $100 Bounty when discharged; also, the chances of Prize Money!

A Soldier who may re-enlist at the expiration of his term of service, will receive $2 per month in addition to his former pay.

A Premium of $2 will be paid immediately to any person bringing an accepted recruit.
Apply at the OFFICE, No. 18 BOWERY.
D. M. COHEN, Capt. Command'g.

BAKER & GODWIN, Printers, Printing-House Square, opposite City Hall, N. Y.

Nor does the USMC have dibs on the *Semper Fidelis* motto, which has been used by any number of noble European families at least as far back as 1180 and is currently the motto of the French cities of Abbeville and St. Malo, the Corsican town of Calvi, Exeter in England, Lviv in Ukraine, and even White Plains, New York. The U.S. Army's Eleventh Infantry Regiment has adopted it, as have the marine corps of

Portugal and the Republic of China (Taiwan), along with the Swiss Grenadiers, the Hungarian Government Guard, the Romanian secret service, and the Submarine Force of the Chilean Navy.

Mayday, S'il Vous Plaît

The universal distress call "Mayday" is a version of a polite French request for help that was thought up by an Englishman. Frederick Stanley Mockford (1897–1962), senior wireless technician at London's Croydon Airport in 1923, was assigned to come up with a distinctive word to signal distress. It had to be brief, unmistakable, and capable of being understood by everyone. At the time, most of London's air traffic originated from Le Bourget Field in Paris. Mockford knew that the French phrase for "come help me" was *venez m'aider*, so he just lopped off the imperative verb and left the reflexive infinitive, *m'aider*, which he rendered into phonetic English as *Mayday*. It stuck. And it has saved countless lives ever since.

Opposite: "Eyes right! Order arms!" A U.S. Marine corporal in dress blues.

In the Rear with the Gear

Ask any combat soldier, and he'll tell you that "headquarters" is one of the great misnomers of wartime. The truth is that all headquarters are really *hindquarters*, planted safely in the rear of a war zone to dispatch and control the personnel actually risking their lives in the line of fire at the real *head* of combat. So it is not surprising that, among themselves, troops often speak of "reporting to hindquarters" or identifying a new officer as having come to the front "straight from hindquarters."

Of course, the anatomical reference is more than a nod to the rearward location of headquarters. It also refers to the disparity between the seat of intelligence, the human brain, and the just plain seat, the human hindquarters. This formulation may have been initially articulated by whoever was the first to mock, sometime in 1862, an expression that the insufferably pretentious and enormously unpopular Union major general John Pope liked to use. He made it his custom to begin all of his written orders with the dateline phrase, "Headquarters in the Saddle." Pretty soon, someone—no one knows who—pointed out that this described to a tee General Pope's chief weakness as a tactical and strategic commander. He made the mistake of locating his headquarters where his hindquarters should have been.

Opposite: Pompous and unpopular, General John Pope was a mediocre commander who (it was said) made the mistake of locating his headquarters "in the saddle," where his hindquarters should have been.

Got Killed?

Death is just another of those "inconvenient truths" most of us look for ways to avoid confronting. Even military men and women, whose very profession is death, churn out one alternative after another to the phrase "got killed." Perhaps the most innocent-sounding of these is "bought the farm," as in "Oh, Joe? Joe bought the farm in Helmand Province."

The phrase is so folksy—and so widely used in the civilian realm—that it's hard to believe it was the military that bequeathed it to us. It came into use during the early days of military aviation when the U.S. Army Air Corps was frequently forced to write checks reimbursing farmers for crops destroyed when some hapless cadet pilot augured into a field. Accidents were common, and farmers living near air bases routinely inflated their reported losses in a bid to get the biggest payday they could. The Air Corps winked at this practice, and assumed that any young aviator who got himself killed had just "bought the farm."

Below: An early U.S. Army Air Corps aviator "buys the farm."

Eberhardt!

Gerrrr-onnn-i-mooooo! The most famous battle cry since the Rebel Yell of the Civil War, this was the shout of World War II U.S. Army paratroops as they launched themselves, one after another, from their rumbling twin-engine C-47 transports.

Was the cry decreed by some historically minded army officer to honor the Apache warrior leader who, time and again, evaded death or captivity during the Indian Wars of the late nineteenth-century American West?

It was not.

In fact, the only "official" jump cry of a U.S. airborne unit was endorsed by Colonel Robert F. Sink, commanding the 506th Infantry Regiment of the 101st Airborne Division. That cry was "Curahee!" A Cherokee word, meaning "Stand Alone," it was also the name of a mountain within the boundaries of Camp Toccoa, Georgia, where the 506th trained before deployment to North Africa and Europe in World War II.

No, the cry of "Geronimo!" first issued from the lips of a lowly private named Aubrey Eberhardt, who, in August 1940, was a member of a parachute test platoon at Fort Benning, Georgia. Back then, more than a year before the United States entered the war, airborne tactics were still highly experimental. On the eve of the army's very first attempt at a mass jump, betting men were taking wagers on just how many would survive the exercise. Seeking to distract his nervous self that evening, Eberhardt accompanied his buddies to the post movie theater, where they saw the 1939 movie *Geronimo*, starring the Native American actor Chief Thundercloud in the title role. (He had already played

Above: Distinctive unit insignia of the 501st Airborne Infantry Regiment.

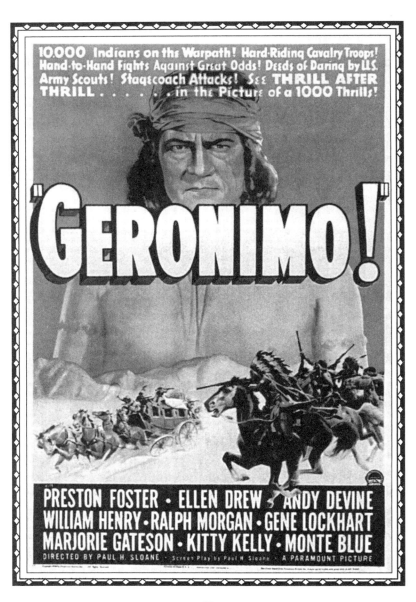

10,000 Indians on the Warpath! Hard-Riding Cavalry Troops! Hand-to-Hand Fights Against Great Odds! Deeds of Daring by U.S. Army Scouts! Stagecoach Attacks! See THRILL AFTER THRILL . . . . . . in the Picture of a 1000 Thrills!

"GERONIMO!"

PRESTON FOSTER · ELLEN DREW · ANDY DEVINE
WILLIAM HENRY · RALPH MORGAN · GENE LOCKHART
MARJORIE GATESON · KITTY KELLY · MONTE BLUE
DIRECTED BY PAUL H. SLOANE · Screen Play by Paul H. Sloane · A PARAMOUNT PICTURE

Tonto in the Republic Pictures *Lone Ranger* serial.) The movie—and a round or two of beers off-post—did the trick for Eberhardt, who smilingly told his comrades-in-arms that tomorrow's jump really wouldn't be all that special after all.

Above: Distinctive unit insignia of the 506th Airborne Infantry Regiment.

One of them snorted in response, betting Eberhardt that he would be so scared he wouldn't be able to remember his own damn name.

"All right, dammit!" Eberhardt exploded. "I tell you jokers what I'm gonna do! To prove to you that I'm not scared out of my wits when I jump, I'm gonna yell 'Geronimo!' loud as hell when I go out that door tomorrow!"

And so he did. Ever since, "Geronimo!" has been the cry of jumpers from airplanes as well as diving boards, and Curahee is nothing more than the name of a mountain known to very few beyond the Georgia town of Toccoa.

Opposite: On this poster for the 1939 movie *Geronimo,* the eponymous Apache chief looms large—but the Native America actor who played him, Chief Thundercloud (born Victor Daniels), goes without billing among the Caucasian "stars."

The Colorblind Leading the Non-Colorblind

Far from providing an often-coveted reason for 4F exemption from the military draft during World War II, colorblindness was a sought-after military asset.

On August 17, 1940, the scientific journal *Nature* published a study showing (among other things) that, in the case of "a building camouflaged with large irregular patches of color, the actual outline of the building may be lost in the jumble of these patterns. But the colorblind person may be scarcely conscious of the variegated colors, so that to him the outline of the building may be almost unaffected by the camouflage."

U.S. and other Allied military medical officers picked up on this, confirmed the results of the study with their own tests, and issued a recommendation that colorblind personnel be specifically identified and deployed to units fighting in the forest lands of Europe as well as the jungles of the Pacific Theater to serve as camouflage spotters.

Lucky Thirteen

By long tradition, the dress blues worn by enlisted U.S. Navy sailors include bell-bottom trousers that have, in place of a zippered fly, a large square front flap secured by thirteen buttons. Officially, the buttons signify the thirteen original states of the Union. Unofficially, they are referred to as "thirteen chances to change your mind."

Opposite: The trousers of this U.S. Navy sailor, part of the landing party attached to the cruiser USS *New York* in 1899, features the traditional thirteen-button trouser fly.

Green Beret Special

President John F. Kennedy enthusiastically championed the development of the U.S. Army's Special Forces as part of what he called the doctrine of "flexible response," an initiative to make the U.S. military more capable of fighting the guerrilla or insurgent wars of the 1960s. He is widely credited with proposing that U.S. Special Forces wear a green beret to distinguish themselves. Although JFK does deserve a big share of the credit, the backstory is a bit more complicated.

The modern U.S. Army Special Forces has its origin in World War II, when the first elite Army Ranger unit, "Darby's Rangers," was created in the summer of 1942. After forming in Northern Ireland, Darby's Rangers received advanced training from British commandos at the Commando Training Depot at Achnacarry Castle, Scotland. The British encouraged the men to wear the bright green beret of a British commando, but U.S. Army brass banned this headgear as a violation of uniform regulations. A decade later, at the end of the Korean War, the U.S. Army's Tenth Special Forces Group (Airborne), which included a large number of World War II Darby vets, casually wore various berets, in crimson, maroon, and black, before "rifle-green" was officially chosen, based on a Canadian Army precedent. When the Tenth wore the new green berets during a 1955 ceremony at Fort Bragg, North Carolina, many in attendance started asking where the "foreign delegation" had come from. A mortified Fort Bragg commandant, General Paul D. Adams, immediately banned the rifle-green beret.

Left: Distinctive unit insignia for the U.S. Special Forces. **Opposite:** Recruiting poster for the Special Forces, circa 1970.

"I always wanted to wear the Green Beret."

Why are you staying in?

See your Career Counselor about the Special Forces Reenlistment Option.

Above: U.S. Navy Rear Admiral Frank Friday Fletcher (right) is pictured in 1915 with his chief of staff, Captain Hues, who sports a set of "loafer's loops" on his left shoulder.

When he was appointed commander of the U.S. Army Warfare Center at Fort Bragg, Brigadier General William P. Yarborough petitioned the Pentagon to reinstate the green beret for Special Forces. His request received no traction until President John F. Kennedy personally intervened, and on September 25, 1961, the Department of the Army issued "Message 578636," designating the green beret as the "exclusive headdress" of the U.S. Army Special Forces. JFK later called it "a symbol of excellence, a badge of courage, a mark of distinction in the fight for freedom."

Badge of Honor?

Officers of special distinction—some would argue, officers with family connections—may be accorded coveted special staff duties as aides to senior government officials or to military officers of flag rank (in other words, generals and admirals). To distinguish their elite office, each of these officers wears an *aiguillette*, a decoratively braided and looped cord. In U.S. military service, presidential aides and aides to other high-ranking civilian officials wear the aiguillette on the right shoulder. Those assigned to military flag officers wear it on the left. Moreover, the number of loops in the aiguillette must equal the number of stars worn by the officer to whom the aide is assigned. Thus aides to four-star generals and admirals (as well as to the U.S. president) get four loops; aides to a lieutenant general or vice admiral get three, because their assigned officer is distinguished by three stars; those assigned to a major general or rear admiral (upper)—a two-star rank—get two; and the aide to a brigadier general or rear admiral (lower) gets just one, to match the single star of that rank.

Some say the unique badge of honor that is the aiguillette originated in a moment of shame. A commander in an unspecified European army, appalled by what he deemed the less-than-valorous conduct of some of his troops, resolved to summarily hang several as an example to the others. The chosen soldiers beseeched their commander to give them one chance to redeem themselves, and they offered to wear a rope and spike over their shoulders, which might be used to hang them on the spot if ever they disappointed their commander again. Less glamorous explanations hold that the aiguillette was originally a rope kept handy to tie the general's horse when he dismounted in the field or was nothing more than a cord to hold a pencil used to write field dispatches.

No one has ever offered persuasive evidence for either of these tales of origin, but American GIs and sailors agree that the aiguillette, more than anything else, reminds them of "chicken guts," which is one nickname for this feature of the Class A uniform in the U.S. military. An alternative designation among ordinary soldiers, sailors, marines, and airmen is "loafer's loops," which also serves as their frank appraisal of the aide's actual function in military life. Whether in the one-, two-, three-, or four-loop variety, by far the largest collection of loafer's loops is to be found in the Five-Sided Squirrel Cage, a nickname for the building otherwise known as the Pentagon, the nation's military headquarters.

Unadorned and Spherical

Women serving in the United States Navy may wear earrings, provided that officers wear gold and enlisted personnel restrict themselves to silver. The U.S. Army allows women of all ranks to wear silver, gold, white pearl, or diamond earrings, provided that they do "not exceed 6 mm or ¼ inch in diameter" and are "unadorned and spherical." Moreover, army earrings must "fit snugly against the ear" and may be worn only "as a matched pair, with just one earring per ear lobe."

Operation Urgent Phone Call

Operation Urgent Fury was a 1983 U.S. military intervention in the Caribbean island nation of Grenada to suppress a Cuban/Soviet-supported radical regime that was potentially imperiling some 1,000 American students attending a local medical college.

The invasion force of some 7,300 U.S. Army Rangers, Eighty-Second Airborne troops, U.S. Marines, and U.S. Special Forces personnel was deployed from a naval battle group led by the aircraft carrier USS *Independence*. On October 25, the force landed. Although no opposition was met on the beach, the Americans, as they advanced inland, encountered 500 to 600 Grenadian regulars, 2,000 to 2,500 ill-equipped Grenadian militiamen, and about 800 Cuban military construction personnel. Brushing aside this inferior opposition, the invasion force successfully evacuated all U.S. nationals without suffering civilian casualties. Eighteen U.S. military personnel were killed in the assault on Grenada, and 116 were wounded, whereas Grenadian forces lost forty-five, with another 358 wounded. Cuban casualties were twenty-five dead and fifty-nine wounded. By November 2, Grenada was declared "secure."

Fearing "liberal media" bias, the Reagan administration had barred journalists from landing with the troops, and no live reporting issued from Grenada until about sixty hours after the operation had begun. This clampdown outraged and alienated reporters, who retaliated by downplaying the success of the operation and almost gleefully reporting its blunders, which included intelligence so inadequate that the invasion force had trouble finding the American medical students and, even more embarrassing, were plagued by extraordinary failures of military communications. As reporters explained, no one had thought to equip the invading forces with integrated, interoperable radios. The units went into combat without even having agreed upon a single set of broadcast frequencies. Marines and Army Rangers were simply unable to talk to one another, and, at one point, a flummoxed member of the force decided to place a commercial long-distance telephone call, collect, to Fort Bragg, North Carolina, so that he could ask commanders there to radio orders to an AC-130 gunship, already in Grenada, to fly a support sortie as his ground troops came under heavy fire.

Below: Flight operations aboard the amphibious assault ship USS *Guam* off the coast of Grenada during Operation Urgent Fury, 1983. Visible on the flight deck are a UH-1N Iroquois (single-rotor helicopter) and a CH-46 Sea King (twin rotor).

Chapter Three

Questionable Strategies, Tenuous Tactics, and Outright Blunders

SNATCHED FROM THE
JAWS OF VICTORY

Advance to the Rear

It sounds counterintuitive, but the most difficult and dangerous maneuver any army is ever called upon to execute is not the advance against a formidable foe, but the retreat from one. Think about it: When you move forward, your weapon is pointed toward the enemy, but in retreat you point it away. The high command of certain armies believed it a cowardly disgrace to train recruits to retreat, so they never bothered. Instead, training was all about the advance and the attack, never the withdrawal. The result was that during World War II Russia, Germany, and Japan often found themselves all shot up with no place to go. The Germans were able to penetrate so deeply into Soviet territory early in the war because the retreating Red Army just did not have a chapter titled "Rearguard Action" in its playbook. When the tables were turned against the Germans during the winter of 1941, and the invaders' advance bogged down outside of Moscow and all along the Eastern Front, it was the Nazis who then discovered they had no clue about defending against a counterattack.

And Japan? In more than a thousand years of its history, Japan had never retreated. In fact, there was no word for *surrender* in the Japanese language. Right up to December 8, 1941, Joseph Grew, U.S. ambassador to Japan, voiced his belief that the Japanese military would never retreat or surrender for the simple reason that it did not know how to do either.

Opposite: A German Panzer Pz Kpw III during the invasion of Russia.

To Kill a President

In the U.S. Civil War, it was apparently okay to kill enemy combatants—new research suggests three-quarters of a million soldiers died in the conflict—but political leaders were considered strictly off-limits. Not that this stopped Brigadier General Judson Kilpatrick from leading a raid on Richmond, Virginia, apparently with the purpose of taking out Confederate president Jefferson Davis and as many of his cabinet as he could get to.

Kilpatrick didn't exactly cut a heroic figure. He was, in 1864, a twenty-eight-year-old West Pointer, short and slight, sporting garish, ginger-colored mutton-chop whiskers and always wearing an outlandishly rakish cavalry hat, a specially tailored cutaway uniform coat that reminded some of the minstrel showman's trademark "swallowtail blue" coat, and buff-colored cavalry trousers tucked into high-topped boots of piratical proportions. As one of his men recalled, "It was hard to look at him without laughing."

And Kilpatrick wasn't just silly *looking*. Vainglorious, he really cared very little about how many of his troops died in pursuit of his dreams. Men under his command, as well as fellow officers, took to calling Kilpatrick "Kilcavalry." General William Tecumseh Sherman had another name for him: "a hell of a damned fool."

By early 1864, the Confederate capital of Richmond was reportedly defended thinly. Seizing on this information, Kilpatrick persuaded his commanding officers to authorize him to make a lightning cavalry raid against Richmond for the

Opposite: Union cavalry forces, 3,585 strong, under the command of Brigadier General Judson Kilpatrick (pictured), set out to liberate prisoners of war at Libby Prison, but quickly ran into trouble as the ill-conceived plan fell apart.

purpose, he said, of harassing Confederate lines of supply and communication, disrupting government, and, most of all, liberating the 5,000 Union prisoners—all officers—languishing in two POW camps, Libby Prison and Belle Isle. Among those thrilled by the prospect of the bold operation was Ulric Dahlgren, who clamored to be named Kilpatrick's second in command. At twenty-one, Dahlgren, who had lost a leg at Gettysburg, was the youngest colonel in the Union army, and the handsome youngster was every bit as dashing as Kilpatrick fancied himself to be. As the son of Rear Admiral John A. Dahlgren, inventor of the famous Dahlgren gun used on most Union warships and many shore installations, he was also very well connected.

Above: Colonel Ulric Dahlgren and 500 of his cavalry troopers ran into stiff resistance at Tunstall's Station. Dahlgren was killed, and more than half of his men were either killed or captured.

The raiding party, consisting of 3,585 troopers, set off at 11 P.M. on February 28, 1864. At Spotsylvania, Virginia, Kilpatrick detached Dahlgren with 500 men to ride along the James River, upstream from Richmond, while he led the main force into Richmond directly from the north. The plan was for Dahlgren to approach from the southwest while Kilpatrick entered from the north, thereby forcing the defenders to divide what was assumed to be an already modest force.

Above: Colonel Ulric Dahlgren—would-be assassin of Jefferson Davis?

It *was* a plan—though it is doubtful that the raiding party Kilpatrick commanded could have overwhelmed even a thinly defended objective. In any case, the plan instantly folded when Dahlgren failed to materialize outside of Richmond. For his part, Kilpatrick encountered much stiffer resistance than he had anticipated and withdrew from the outskirts of the capital, in the process stumbling into the 260 survivors of Dahlgren's detachment at a place called Tunstall's Station, near the Pamunkey River. Dahlgren, they told him, was dead, and almost half his command had been killed or captured.

Following pages: Brigadier General Judson Kilpatrick (fourth from left) and his staff at Stevensburg, Virginia, March 1864, near the scene of the Battle of Brandy Station. Colonel Ulric Dahlgren is standing next to the steps, second from right.

And so the "Kilpatrick-Dahlgren Raid" might have been chalked up as yet another of the Civil War's many reckless and failed military ventures were it not for a handwritten speech, penned on official Third Division stationery, that the Confederates found in Dahlgren's pocket:

> You have been selected from brigades and regiments as a picked command to attempt a desperate undertaking….
>
> We hope to release the prisoners from Belle Island first, and, having seen them fairly started, we will cross the James river into Richmond, destroying the bridges after us, and exhorting the released prisoners to destroy and burn the hateful city, and do not allow the Rebel leader, Davis, and his traitorous crew to escape…. Jeff Davis and Cabinet [are to be] killed….

The shocking document was conveyed to President Davis, who immediately sent it to the Richmond newspapers for publication as evidence of the depths of Northern treachery. Gentlemen did not resort to assassination!

In response to the newspaper stories and official protests from the Confederacy, Dahlgren's and Kilpatrick's superiors disavowed any knowledge of an assassination plot, and while no Federal conspiracy to assassinate the Confederate president has ever been proved, neither has one been conclusively disproved. The official objectives of the Kilpatrick-Dahlgren Raid are a matter of historical record. Whether there was an unofficial agenda of assassination remains a mystery of the Civil War, but those who knew Judson "Kilcavalry" Kilpatrick were not surprised by—and did not question—the document published in the Richmond papers.

Above: Dahlgren's men defend against determined Confederate resistance during the Kilpatrick Raid.

A Civil War 9/11

During the Civil War, Confederate agents went north to conduct espionage, rob banks, and raid towns and farms. Particularly ambitious attempts to create chaos and instigate popular uprisings were set for November 8, 1864: election day in the Union. These attacks were to target Chicago, Cincinnati, towns throughout Missouri and Iowa, and, in particular, New York City. The Chicago operation was aborted as Union counterintelligence rooted out the scheme, and, with the failure of the Chicago uprising, the planned revolts elsewhere likewise collapsed. But three die-hard agents—Colonel Robert Martin and Lieutenant John W. Headley (both former subordinates of the famed Rebel raider John Hunt Morgan), plus a shadowy figure known only as Captain Longuemare from Missouri—refused to be discouraged and decided to act on their own. Their plan was to organize other operatives to check into New York City's nineteen most prominent hotels. Each man would go up to his room, set it on fire, calmly walk out, and let the whole building burn. They confidently assumed that these fires would spread throughout the mostly frame-built New York and devastate the city.

From a compliant chemist in Greenwich Village, Longuemare ordered 144 four-ounce bottles of what was called Greek fire—an incendiary weapon dating to the Byzantine Empire and believed to have been compounded (in the nineteenth century) of some combination of pine resin, quicklime, naphtha, sulfur, and possibly saltpeter. Headley picked up the Greek fire from the chemist and loaded all 144 bottles into a carpetbag valise. From Greenwich Village, he had to transport it to a Confederate safe house near Central Park, which, in 1864, was still under development. Lugging the valise, he boarded a horse-drawn streetcar, tucking the weighty bag between his legs. As the conveyance lurched along the tracks, Headley detected the rotten-egg stench of hydrogen sulfide. He looked down at the valise, expecting to see a telltale puddle of Greek fire. But all was safely dry.

Then a fellow passenger, a woman, made a loud sniffing noise. "Something smells dead here!" she called out. "Conductor, something smells dead in that man's valise!"

Headley must have felt a wave of panic. Yet nobody else in the car stirred. The Confederate hastened to leave the streetcar, trudged the rest of the way to the safe house, and distributed the bottles to his fellow operatives. This done, he and the other agents left the house. Beginning about seven o'clock in the evening, they registered at the hotels.

Each man signed in, received his key, walked up to his room, and closed the door. Headley later related what he had done at the Astor House: "I hung the bedclothes loosely on the headboard and piled the chairs, drawers of the bureau, and washstand on the bed, then stuffed some newspapers about among the mass and poured a bottle of turpentine over it all." Instead of hurling the bottle of Greek fire against the wall, which would have exploded, attracting immediate attention, he just spilled it on a "pile of rubbish. It blazed up instantly and the whole bed seemed to be in flames before I could get out. I locked the door and...left the key at the office as usual." After walking through the lobby with calm deliberation, he went off to register at the City Hotel, his next target. Then he set off on a stroll along the West Side wharves, hurling bottles of Greek fire at a number of vessels tied up there.

Very soon, rumors of a rebel invasion buzzed through the streets of Manhattan as two floors of the Belmont Hotel and the Metropolitan were destroyed and the St. Nicholas was totally engulfed, a complete loss. A dry goods firm was gutted, and a few ships were damaged. In addition to the hotels, the arsonists hit the famed Barnum's Museum on lower Broadway, creating a blaze made all the more terrifying by the roar of lions and tigers and the trumpeting of elephants trapped in their cages. The flames drove Barnum's seven-foot-tall giantess into a frenzy and required five strong firemen and a physician's sedative to bring her under control. Yet the citywide conflagration the conspirators had anticipated did not break out.

No one knows for certain why all of Manhattan failed to explode into flame. Possibly, the Greenwich Village chemist had prepared a weak batch of Greek fire. More likely, most of the fires in the hotel rooms had burned out too quickly, because none of the arsonists had thought to open a window to feed the flames. The fires rapidly consumed all the available oxygen in the closed rooms and guttered out before they could spread. Whatever the cause of the ultimately underwhelming attempt at terrorism, the disheartened conspirators fled back to refuge in Canada. As the fires died in New York, so, too, did the last of the major Confederate terrorist conspiracies.

Opposite: Illustration from *Harper's Weekly* showing a Confederate agent setting a fire in New York City.

Killer Beef

America's war with Spain in 1898 was the first time the U.S. Army had ever fought overseas, and it was totally unprepared for large-scale offensive operations offshore. Officials scrambled to cobble together transportation to Cuba and the Philippines, where the war was being fought, and also to provision the army. President McKinley's secretary of war, Russell A. Alger, rushed through contracts with Chicago's meatpacking giants, Morris & Co., Swift & Co., and Armour & Co., to supply refrigerated bulk meat as well as canned meat in large quantities at rock-bottom prices. The result was the shipment of a massive amount of inferior beef that had been improperly refrigerated in bulk, improperly preserved in canning, and adulterated with harsh chemicals in an effort to retard or at least disguise spoilage. Most of the meat shipped to Cuba was, beyond question, unfit for consumption. Soldiers aptly called it "embalmed beef."

Most historians believe that the meat, either dangerously spoiled or chemically toxic, killed twice as many Americans as Spanish bullets did. This is almost certainly true, although no records of foodborne illness, especially dysentery, were kept, and, indeed, endemic yellow fever and malaria were so common in Cuba that even mild cases of food poisoning were likely to prove fatal. Nevertheless, the quality of the meat was so bad that a court of inquiry was convened. Commanding General Nelson A. Miles presented the court with a letter from an army medical officer, who wrote that much "of the [bulk] beef I examined arriving on the transports from the United States...[was] apparently preserved by injected chemicals to aid deficient refrigeration." He observed that, although it "looked well," this meat "had an odor similar to that of a dead human body after being injected with formaldehyde, and it tasted when first cooked like decomposed boric acid."

Above: The chaos on the Tampa, Florida, docks was the result of a total failure of U.S. Army logistics at the outset of the Spanish-American War.

The canned meat, Miles testified, wasn't much better. He cited a description from one regimental colonel, who observed that the "meat...soon became putrid" when the cans were opened. In fact, "in many of the cans [it] was found [already] in course of putrefaction when opened."

Impatient with a court of inquiry unwilling to offend the politically powerful meat packers, Miles went directly to the press, claiming that the canned meat was in reality a by-product of the process for making beef extract. "There was no life or nourishment in the meat," the general declared. "It had been used to make beef extract, and after the juice was squeezed out of it the pulp was put back in the cans and labeled 'roast beef.'" A self-righteous scandal exploded and, ultimately, Secretary of War Alger was forced to step down. The U.S. Army would, however, again be plagued by sub-par meat rations during World War I—supplied at cut rate by the same big packing companies.

Below: General Nelson Miles with his staff officers in Cuba, 1898.

Nuclear Mission

The Danish physicist Niels Bohr (1885–1962), who won a Nobel Prize for figuring out the structure of the atom, was trapped in his native country during World War II —a fact that began to weigh heavily on the Americans and their British allies as they raced to beat the Nazis to the building of an atomic bomb. Figuring it would be a good thing to snatch for the Allied team the man who had explained the atom, the British launched a super-secret operation to extract Bohr from his home in Copenhagen. Unfortunately, German counterintelligence learned of the rescue plan and came knocking at Bohr's front door even as the scientist was making for the back exit during the rescue. Bohr paused just long enough to snatch a beer bottle that he had filled with "heavy water," water enriched with the hydrogen isotope deuterium, at the time essential to the operation of some nuclear reactors.

Bottle in hand, Bohr made his escape while Danish resistance fighters opened fire on the pursuing Germans, managing to hold them off just long enough for the fifty-eight-year-old scientist to be ushered onto a fishing boat and transported to Sweden. He was covertly transferred by way of Stockholm to a makeshift airstrip in a clearing hacked out of the woods. There, a diminutive RAF Mosquito fighter-bomber—two high-performance engines mounted on a mostly wooden airframe—picked him up and flew him to England. The Mosquito soared to some 20,000 feet when, suddenly, Bohr's oxygen supply failed. Noticing that his passenger was out cold, the quick-thinking pilot rapidly descended, but Bohr remained unconscious and could not be revived until he reached a Scottish hospital—a death grip still wrapped around his beer bottle.

Bohr recovered and was flown to the United States, where he joined the Manhattan Project, the top-secret effort to make an atomic bomb. By this time, however, most of the major theoretical problems had been solved, and Bohr contributed little to the creation of the two weapons that were dropped in 1945 on Hiroshima and Nagasaki.

As for the heavy water—a substance of great value—it turned out to be beer. Bohr had grabbed the wrong bottle.

Puddle Pirates

It's no secret that personnel of the U.S. Navy have a low opinion of personnel of the U.S. Coast Guard, whom they deride as "Brown Water Sailors" and "Puddle Pirates." During the Prohibition era, from roughly 1920 to 1933, rum running was so common a practice that the U.S. Coast Guard, hard pressed to patrol the inlets and small ports by which illegal liquor entered the country, recruited every man who possessed both a willingness to join up and a pulse. Most actively sought were rejects from the other military services, especially the U.S. Navy. Men who had been discharged as "undesirable," who had exhibited criminal tendencies, or who had committed actual crimes, but who were not sufficiently felonious to warrant outright dishonorable discharge, were embraced by the Coast Guard and installed on the next available cutter. Little wonder that navy, marine, and army men took to calling the Coast Guard the "Hooligan Navy." Yet these "hooligans" often found themselves in a shooting war with well-armed rum runners, and, to this day, Coast Guard personnel wear the slur "Hooligan Navy" as a badge of honor.

Above: U.S. Coast Guardsmen of the cutter *Seneca* interdict a Prohibition-era rumrunner.

Scratch My Back, But Don't Blow Me Up

Tanks are very good at killing people and breaking things. Nevertheless, back in the day when their top speed was in the low double digits, they were vulnerable to infantry attack by soldiers who ran alongside and jumped aboard a slow-moving tank. Once on the vehicle's deck, they attempted to breach a hatch and toss in a grenade or to plant a grenade or sticky bomb in the wheels and tracks. When the crew of one tank would sight such an attempt against a brother tank, they directed raking machine-gun fire against those trying to board. Such fire was called "back scratching." Unlike its namesake, however, which describes a generally pleasurable experience, back scratching a tank with machine-gun fire can have unintended consequences. In the case of the U.S. Army's World War II-era Sherman tank, which was thinly armored and ran on highly explosive gasoline rather than more stable diesel fuel, a stray round could easily blow up the "friendly," together with everyone inside.

Frag You, Sir

Judging from both official and unofficial reports, one of the most popular pastimes in the U.S. Army of the Vietnam era was *fragging*. The word is derived from the antipersonnel fragmentation grenade and refers to the assassination of an unpopular fellow soldier—usually a company or other small-unit commander who makes it a habit to order his men into harm's way. During the Vietnam War, 230 fatal fragging cases were thoroughly documented, and an additional 1,400 officer deaths have never been explained and are widely attributed to fragging. In the two-year period 1970–1971, 363 assaults "with explosive devices" were recorded against U.S. Army officers in Vietnam.

Actually attempting to blow someone up is hardly a low-profile crime, but simply saluting an officer at the wrong time and in the wrong place may be so low-profile as to be classified as a kind of stealth assassination. The seemingly innocuous act of saluting a superior on an active battlefield is considered worse than bad form because it instantly identifies the officer. To any enemy snipers watching, it marks a target—so effectively, in fact, that a battlefield salute is known as a "sniper check."

Is such a salute in such a time and place merely thoughtless? Or is it murder? Who knows? But it certainly happens.

Bargain Basement Armageddon

After August 1945, when the United States ended World War II with atomic bombs dropped on the Japanese cities of Hiroshima and Nagasaki, most of the world saw nuclear weapons as ultimate weapons—not just war-winning, but civilization-ending. Those at the top of the U.S. defense establishment, however, regarded them as something else. They thought of them as military bargains.

No one denied, of course, that it was expensive to build atomic bombs and, later, missiles with nuclear and thermonuclear warheads. It was, however, much cheaper than maintaining, equipping, and deploying a vast *conventional* (non-nuclear) army, navy, and air force. The promise of nuclear weapons was encapsulated in a doctrine called *mutual assured destruction*, known by the acronym "MAD." MAD described the understanding between nuclear adversaries that if one side used the weapons, the other side would retaliate in kind, thereby assuring Armageddon and making even the prospect of a Third World War unthinkable. For this reason, it was argued, a massive atomic stockpile, a "credible nuclear deterrent," made creating and paying for a large conventional force unnecessary. Given the prospect of MAD, no one would ever actually start a war.

And so, U.S. military planners claimed that a high-tech nuclear arsenal, packing enough destructive force to wipe out world civilization many times over, was the military deal of a lifetime—billions of lifetimes, in fact. President Dwight D. Eisenhower's secretary of defense, Charles Erwin Wilson (1953–1957), said that investing in nuclear and thermonuclear weapons gave the nation "more bang for the buck" than equipping "conventional" (non-nuclear) forces. Dollar for dollar, the nukes provided more of a deterrent as well as more destructive potential. Somewhere in the bowels of the Pentagon, however, a military analyst wryly observed that Secretary Wilson's USSR counterpart was undoubtedly making the equivalent argument in favor of a *Soviet* strategic weapons stockpile, claiming that it would deliver "more rubble per ruble."

Opposite: Most WW II U.S. Army Air Forces bombers were painted a drab brown-green with "cloud-gray" on the underside, like these B-17s. **Following pages:** The B-24 Liberator, however, is painted in the outlandish pattern of a "Judas goat," to better lead the formation to its target.

Follow the Leader

Holding high the national or regimental colors at the head of a column charging into desperate battle was traditionally regarded as one of the great honors of war. By the time World War II—producer of some 73 million corpses—rolled around, the "honor" had understandably fallen out of favor—at least in the U.S. Army Air Forces.

Some 619,020 U.S. airmen were assigned to carry out or support the strategic bombing of Germany and German-held targets throughout Europe. Of this number, 79,265 were lost in action—mostly shot down by antiaircraft fire and encounters with enemy fighter planes. In an effort to more effectively defend against fighters, the bombing missions were carefully planned around tight formations of B-17s or B-24s following a designated lead aircraft, which was always brightly and distinctively painted. The plane whose crew had the "honor" of this assignment was universally known as the "Judas goat." It was a phrase borrowed from the stockyards, where goats were trained to lead sheep or cattle to loading pens for rail transportation to the slaughterhouse or, sometimes, directly through the slaughterhouse doors. As Judas Iscariot betrayed the Lamb of God to crucifixion, so too did these "Judas goats" betray their four-legged brethren to the blades of the abattoir. As a Judas goat led lambs to slaughter, so too did the parti-colored lead bombers betray their comrades into the thick of enemy antiaircraft defenses and fighter attack.

10-2-4

Longtime fans of Dr. Pepper fondly remember the soft drink's famous bottle cap, which featured the somewhat cryptic numbers 10, 2, and 4 deployed as on the face of a clock. Back in the 1940s, the company developed an ad campaign promoting "Dr. Pepper Time"—ten, two, and four o'clock, the prescribed hours at which one was supposed to loosen the ol' tool belt, have a seat, put one's feet up, and suck down a refreshing bottle of the Doctor. The campaign and the concept caught on, and, during World War II, Dr. Pepper sponsored a radio show at first called *The 10-2-4 Ranch* and then *10-2-4 Time*.

Fast forward to another war, this one in Vietnam, where U.S. Air Force and Navy pilots were getting their tails whipped by an alarmingly effective North Vietnamese surface-to-air missile (SAM) tactic by which three SAMs were fired at an aircraft simultaneously, one from the ten o'clock position (with respect to the target), one from the two o'clock, and one from the four o'clock: 10, 2, and 4. The pilots called such an attack a *Dr. Pepper*.

☆ ☆ ☆

Chapter Four

Weapons, Widgets, and Weirdness

SOME STRANGE
THINGS ABOUT
THE INSTRUMENTS
OF WAR

Oldest Weapon?

Based on archaeological evidence, people were making stone clubs as early as the Paleolithic (Old Stone) Age, at least 10,000 years ago. This weapon was the direct ancestor of the mace, which is essentially a club with spikes added, the earliest examples of which were used in ancient Egypt some 6,000 years ago. The club and its reincarnation as the mace get our vote for the oldest weapon known to military history.

Build It, and They Will Leave

During the series of conflicts of conquest known as the Gallic Wars (58–51 BCE), Julius Caesar labored mightily to subdue the fierce tribes in and around Gaul. After his Romans had defeated the mighty Nervii, the most feared of the Belgic warriors, the other peoples of Gaul either actively aligned themselves with Rome or simply ceased all resistance.

There was one notable exception. The Aduatuci were a Germanic tribe that originated in Jutland but lived, by the first century BCE, like the Nervii themselves, in the eastern portion of what is today eastern Belgium. They were descended from the fearsome Cimbri, Teutones, and Ambrones tribes. When they heard of the defeat of the Nervii, they decided to abandon (in Caesar's words, from his own historic masterpiece, *The Gallic Wars*) "all their towns and forts" and gather "all their stuff in one stronghold, which was admirably fortified by Nature" on what is today the Meuse River.

Opposite: In 1842, the German artist Friedrich Martin von Reibisch rendered this concept of the moveable siege tower Caesar used to intimidate the Aduatuci in the siege of Namur, 57 BCE.

Caesar described the Aduatuci fortress town as looking "down over the steep-est rocks" on every side of its circumference. On "one side only was left a gently sloping approach, not more than two hundred feet in breadth." The Aduatuci had fortified this narrow incline "with a double wall of great height," and they were in the process of "setting stones of great weight and sharpened beams upon the wall" to make it even more impregnable.

Caesar's legions set up camp nearby. The Aduatuci "made frequent sallies from the stronghold, and engaged in petty encounters with our troops." They dared not, however, emerge in large numbers from their fortress town for an all-out, show-down battle. Accordingly, Caesar responded with industrious patience.

Caesar ordered his men to set about building around the entire Aduatuci stronghold (except for the side that abutted the Meuse River itself) what he described as a "fortified rampart of fifteen thousand feet in circumference, with forts at close intervals." This surrounding wall engulfed the enemy fortress, cutting it off completely.

As Caesar's great wall drew to completion, the Aduatuci remained holed up in their town, comforting themselves (according to Caesar) with the thought that the strength of mere men—especially Romans of puny stature compared with the "huge physique" of the Gauls—could never hope to breach their walls. But Caesar ordered his engineers to build a siege tower, a colossal structure on massive wheels, which could be pulled into position against the enemy's wall and used as a covered platform from which archers and ballista men—who operated massive "ballista" catapults—could fire their missiles over the enemy's walls.

The Aduatuci had failed to imagine the extraordinary mobility of the great tower. Its beautifully constructed wheels made the most out of the combined strength of men and animals. In the end, Julius Caesar never even had to begin actual bombardment from his tower. The mere sight of the awesome structure *actually in motion* terrified the tribesmen. As soon as the tower started to roll, they hurriedly sent emissaries to sue for peace. These ambassadors told Caesar that, obviously, the Romans waged war with divine aid, "inasmuch as they could move forward at so great a speed engines of so great a height." Having thus beheld the power of Caesar, the Aduatuci "submitted themselves and all they had to the power of Rome."

☆ ☆ ☆

Left Over Right, Right?

Ever wonder why women's blouses button right over left, but men's shirts button left over right? It started in the days of the sword. Right-handed men—which was and still is most of them—hung their swords over their left hip, so that it could be drawn by reaching over the torso with the right hand. By buttoning the shirt, vest, or coat left over right, the swordsman, as he drew his weapon, was certain not to snag the hilt or guard on the edge of the fabric—something that could have been disastrous to the garment and catastrophic to the wearer. Women didn't wear swords, so they had no such concerns.

Bell-Bottom Buoys

The bell-bottomed trousers traditionally worn by sailors in several national navies were adopted mainly to make it easy for the lads to take their trousers off without having to pause to untie their shoes—an especially valuable expedient when evacuating a rapidly sinking ship. However, the really smart sailors were not supposed to leave their pants behind when they abandoned ship. They were told that, by tying off the wide cuffs in tight knots, they could trap enough air in the pant legs to make the garment serve as an improvised life preserver. At least, that was the theory. No anecdotal evidence exists for its actual application.

Opposite: Seaman apprentice, in bell-bottoms, aboard the battleship USS *Vermont* during the Spanish-American War, 1898.

Brown Bess

Officially, the British Royal Army referred to it as the "Long Land Pattern Service Musket," but soldiers called it the "Brown Bess," which was the familiar and still famous name for most firelock muskets of the eighteenth century, including those used by British and American forces in the American Revolution.

No one knows for certain where the name came from. The origin of the "Brown" part might seem easy enough to guess, since the walnut gunstock was naturally brown; however, it was usually painted black. As for "Bess," the origin is even more obscure. Some have guessed that it was a reference to Queen Elizabeth I. But she reigned from 1558 to 1603, and the Long Land Pattern Service Musket did not enter service until more than a century after her death. Still others claim the weapon was named after a legendary highwayman who held up stagecoaches with a musket and rode a horse he called Black Bess. Linguists have another answer. They say that "Bess" is an Anglicized corruption of the Dutch *buss*, meaning gun barrel, or, perhaps, of the German *Büchse*, meaning gun.

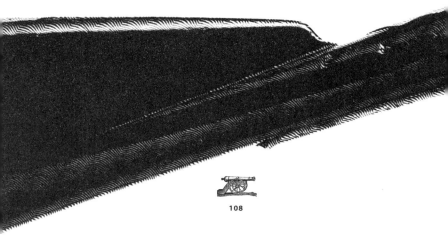

Those who believe they know how soldiers think insist that the musket is called Bess because a good soldier always thinks of his primary weapon in intimate terms—much as he would a wife or lover. And it is true that, even today, fighting men are encouraged to bestow on their rifle the name of their girlfriend or even their mother.

Whether a wife, lover, or mother, the musket of the American Revolution was a demanding mistress. The eighteenth-century British Manual of Arms prescribed no fewer than a dozen precise motions for loading, aiming, firing, and reloading the Brown Bess, all of which procedures had to be performed under fire and from a standing position. The reasonably well-trained soldier could hope to get through

Above: Hammer and lock from a Brown Bess musket used by the British army during the American Revolution. This weapon was carried during the Battle of Bunker Hill by a soldier in the Light Company of the 5th Regiment.

all twelve steps sufficiently fast to squeeze off two shots a minute. A really superb soldier might get off as many as five shots in those same sixty seconds. But that was exceptional, and a scared soldier might never even load his musket, let alone shoot it. Even worse, he might ram down one load after another without firing. When he finally did pull the trigger, the overloaded weapon would explode, killing or injuring the shooter as well as those closest to him.

The heavy demands imposed by the Brown Bess dictated many of the most basic tactics of warfare during the period of the American Revolution. Armies with muskets relied on massed fire rather than individual sharpshooting. What is more, their commanders understood that the first massed volley fired was invariably the most effective. The muskets were muzzle-loaders, which were awkward to load properly. Before the first shot was fired, troops had all the time in the world to load their powder and their bullet carefully enough to ensure that both were properly tamped down with the ramrod. Once the fighting really got under way, however, musket fire became decreasingly reliable, especially when soldiers had their fourteen-inch bayonets fixed in place (this made wielding the ramrod and shoving it down the barrel very awkward indeed). As the battle became more desperate and reloading more feverish, shooting became even less effective. Many muskets misfired or propelled the ball at a lower velocity, which meant it was both less accurate and less destructive.

It is a wonder that eighteenth-century armies managed to kill as efficiently as they did. Doubtless, this is because experienced officers left little to chance. The ideal was to transform frightened men into unthinking components of an

Previous pages: Battle of Bunker Hill, June 17, 1775. A British officer's idea for the perfect soldier was to transform frightened men into unthinking components of an unfeeling machine.

unfeeling machine. Troops were arrayed on the firing line in two or three ranks. After the front rank fired, its men, with crisp movements, retired behind the second—or third—rank to reload. As they reloaded, what had been the second row fired, and while it reloaded, the third (if there was one) fired—by which time the original front row had rotated back to the front, and, having reloaded, fired again. None of this was expected to come off spontaneously. Each movement—loading, ramming, cocking, priming the pan, and firing—came in response to an order barked by a sergeant or an officer. If the machine was working the way it should, a volley was fired every fifteen seconds. The winner of an engagement between two armies of musket men was the one that had the most soldiers sufficiently well trained to fire, reload, and fire again most quickly and accurately. It was a matter of mathematics, mechanics, and, of course, blood.

☆ ☆ ☆

Shoe-In

The word "sabotage," along with the basic concept it signifies, was borrowed from *sabot*, the French word for the wooden clogs traditionally worn by French farmers and laborers. Some etymologists believe the word came from the practice of discontented millworkers, who would remove their sabots and use them to jam the gears of windmills that ground corn and other grains. Others, including the editors of the much-esteemed *Oxford English Dictionary*, find a more specific and recent origin for "sabotage" in a tactic used during a French railway strike of 1910, in which "sabots"—the name applied to the wooden "shoes" that held track rails in place—were deliberately removed to cause derailments.

Saddle and Sword

As generals, George Brinton McClellan, commander of the Union's Army of the Potomac in the Civil War, and George Smith Patton Jr., commander of the Third U.S. Army in World War II, would seem to have nothing in common other than their first names. Whereas McClellan was pathologically cautious and so reluctant to fight that Abraham Lincoln diagnosed him as being afflicted with a bad "case of the slows," Patton led his Third Army with great speed into the heart of Nazi-held Europe. His forces killed more of the enemy and liberated more civilian territory in less time than any other comparably manned and equipped military formation in World War II. Even the formidable German field marshal Gerd von Rundstedt told his Allied captors at the end of the war that "Patton was your best."

Yet both the dithering McClellan and the dynamic Patton were equally successful as military inventors. In April 1855, a half-dozen years before the Civil War,

Above: Twenty-eight-year-old Captain George B. McClellan, at right, was assigned a plum position in the U.S. military commission sent to observe the Crimean War (1855–1856). The other commission members are ordnance expert Alfred Mordecai (seated, left) and the commission head, Richard Delafield (seated, right), U.S. Army engineer and former West Point superintendent. The unidentified man standing second from left is presumably a Russian army officer.

the U.S. War Department sent Captain McClellan to Europe as part of a U.S. Army commission to study the latest in European tactics, weaponry, and logistics employed in fighting the Crimean War. Among the many recommendations McClellan brought back home with him was a design for a cavalry saddle he described as his own modification of a Hungarian type used by Prussian forces. Many recent scholars argue that the design was actually modified from the so-called Spanish tree saddle, which McClellan would have seen in Mexico during the U.S.-Mexican War of 1846–1848. No matter, McClellan's proposed design was adopted by the War Department in 1859 and proved so popular with troopers that it remained standard issue for the United States Cavalry until it was disbanded as an army branch in 1951.

Patton, who would become most famous as one the army's great tactical innovators, particularly in his early advocacy and mastery of armored (tank) warfare in both World War I and World War II, nevertheless reveled in military history and tradition. He even believed that he had fought as a soldier in multiple incarnations throughout history, including as a Roman legionnaire and a soldier of Napoleon. In 1912, the army gave him leave to compete in the modern pentathlon at the Olympics held in Stockholm. Placing fifth overall, he was singled out by the Swedish press for his "calm," "unusual," and "calculated" swordsmanship, which exploited "his opponent's every weakness." Inspired by his own performance, Patton traveled to the French army's cavalry school at Saumur, where the world-renowned instructor known to history only as Adjutant Cléry gave him two weeks of private fencing lessons. When Second Lieutenant Patton returned to Fort Myer, he had earned sufficient celebrity to merit a dinner invitation from Army Chief of Staff General Leonard Wood.

Below: The "McClellan saddle," seen here, was adopted by the U.S. War Department in 1859.

After Saumur, Patton sat down to compose a long analytical report on the military use of the saber, emphasizing the fact that the French favored thrusting with the weapon when they attacked, using the point of the sword, whereas the Americans slashed with it, using the blade edge rather than the point. In his paper, Patton argued that the thrust came nearer to the spirit of the attack than the slash because it brought the cavalryman into faster, more intimate, and more violent contact with the enemy. He therefore advocated adopting the French approach, which, he wrote, would make American cavalrymen more aggressive.

He did acknowledge, however, that the curved U.S. Army saber in use at the time had been designed for slashing rather than thrusting. He therefore proposed that the army adopt a new, straight design, far better suited to the thrust. Published in the *Cavalry Journal*, the article caused tremendous excitement throughout what was then a small and tightly knit army community. Early in 1913, the secretary of war, Henry Stimson, personally directed the army chief of staff to order the chief of ordinance to manufacture 20,000 new cavalry swords precisely following the pattern Second Lieutenant Patton had drawn up. To this day, the "Patton sword" (U.S. Army Saber, M1913) is the army standard.

Opposite: Colonel George S. Patton Jr. commanded the 5th Cavalry, from July 24, 1938, to December 5, 1938. **Right:** The M1913 Cavalry Saber, designed by Patton.

Ahoy, Landship!

The armored tracked vehicle called a "tank" has nothing to do with containing or carrying liquids, so why is it called a tank?

Dive into the genesis of the vehicle, and you will find it more waterlogged than you would ever have guessed. The fact is that this war-changing, war-winning, *land-based* fighting vehicle was pretty much invented not by an army but by the British Royal Navy, which originally referred to tanks as "landships."

Early in World War I, British army officers were desperately trying to think up ways to break the stalemate on the Western Front, which had quickly frozen into opposing lines of static trenches stretching from the English Channel to the border of neutral Switzerland. Fighting from these fixed positions, which were not only dug in but defended by obstacles and barbed wire, neither side was decisively winning, but both sides were losing—losing men, materiél, and the national will to keep on killing. Finally, someone in the British army got the idea of developing armored vehicles based on the caterpillar tractor already in use in various civilian applications and, in the army itself, to pull heavy guns. The argument in favor of such a vehicle was that its armor would be impervious to the rifle and machine-gun fire that forced infantrymen to hunker down in their trenches and that its caterpillar tracks would allow it to roll over barbed wired, trenches, shell holes, and other obstacles impassable by wheeled vehicles. Despite this highly reasonable reasoning, the tradition-encrusted army high command rejected the proposal out of hand.

In the meantime, however, officers of the Royal Navy Air Service, whose men had been driving armored cars in and around airfields, picked up on the idea, and First Lord of the Admiralty Winston Churchill listened to them. He saw the stalemate-breaking potential of a vehicle capable of climbing over all impediments, and immediately created what he dubbed the "Landships Committee" on February 20, 1915. In September of that year, the committee produced its first design prototype, "Little Willie." It was followed in January 1916 by a larger and more practical vehicle called "Mother."

Throughout 1916, the vehicles were refined and became increasingly practical. As they evolved, the Admiralty decided to change their name from "landships" to something less ostentatious and more conducive to secrecy, lest they tip their hand to the enemy. According to some historians, the factory workmen assigned to assemble tank hulls were told that they were building mobile water tanks for the army. According to others, it was a British army lieutenant colonel,

Below: British Mark I tank, about 1916.

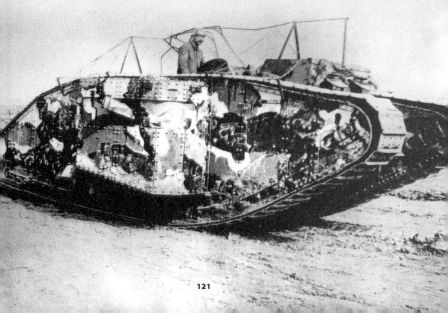

Ernest Swinton, who started calling the vehicles "tanks" in his progress reports to Churchill. Sir Martin Gilbert, Churchill's best modern biographer, observes that manufacturing plans for the vehicles were initially captioned "water carriers for Russia"—again, to preserve secrecy. At some point, somebody in the Admiralty or War Office pointed out that this would sooner or later get shortened to "WCs for Russia." *WC*, of course, is the British acronym for *water closet*—in other words, toilet. The idea that His Majesty's government was making toilets for the Czar's army was an indignity to be avoided at all costs; therefore, according to Gilbert, the drawings

Below: Here, a World War II M-4 Sherman (aka "Ronson") does what it too often did, bursting into flame when hit by enemy fire. **Opposite:** A World War I recruiting poster for the U.S. Tank Corps.

were hurriedly relabeled "water tanks for Russia." From that moment on, the designation "tank" stuck. Although the operational connection between the navy and the tank has long since faded from memory, the nomenclature of tanks still reflects the vehicle's birth at sea, as it were. The underbody of the tank is a "hull," floors are "decks," internal walls or dividers are "bulkheads," and ceilings are "overheads."

While we're talking tanks, we might note that, during World War II, soldiers of the U.S. Army gave that service's main battle tank, the M-4 Sherman, a brand-new moniker. They called it the "Ronson." The nickname was far from affectionate. The Shermans were not heavily armored, and they ran on highly flammable gasoline rather than the less-volatile diesel fuel the Germans used in their Panzers. The combination of light armor and combustible gas meant that an M-4 would explode into flame almost whenever an enemy round penetrated anything vital. With the gallows humor typical of the American GI, Sherman crews took to calling their tanks "Ronsons"—a reference to the popular products of the Ronson Cigarette Lighter Company, whose ads proudly proclaimed: "They light up every time."

Bombs (*Ugh*) Away!

French aircraft designers during World War I specified the use of pure, thin castor oil—that super-slick laxative mothers have been forcing down the unwilling gullets of their backed-up children since time immemorial—for lubricating the high-performance engines of their warplanes. It worked great. Unfortunately for aviators sitting in the era's open cockpits, however, the engine exhaust, heavy with an aerosol of castor oil, blew back into the mouth and nose, often triggering among pilots violent diarrhea in midflight.

Below: A French fighter plane, after crashing into a barn. Could the cause have been pilot error induced by the urgent action of castor oil?

A Most Refreshing Improvised Incendiary Weapon

So-called "petrol bombs"—two-pound glass jam jars filled with gasoline and wrapped with part of a blanket for a wick—were used by Republican troops against Nationalist (Fascist) tanks in the Spanish Civil War of 1936–1939. It was, however, the Winter War of November 1939–March 1940, fought between the invading Soviets and the defending Finns, that gave this device the name by which it is still known today: the Molotov Cocktail.

The name originated with the Finns, who used long-necked bottles instead of jars and, for a fuse, a long wooden storm match instead of a rag. The fuel was not simple gasoline, but a mixture of gasoline, kerosene, tar, and potassium chlorate, which produced an explosive as well as an incendiary effect. The name was a response to a public statement issued by the Soviet People's Commissar for Foreign Affairs, Vyacheslav Molotov, whom Winston Churchill once described as possessing a "cannon-ball head, black moustache,...comprehending eyes,...slab face,... verbal adroitness and imperturbable demeanour." The Red Army, Molotov protested, was by no means *invading* Finland. It was, on the contrary, delivering food to the starving Finns. The Finns countered by announcing that they had prepared a "Molotov Cocktail" to go along with the Soviet-provided meal. Some authorities add that the name was also in response to what the Soviet Red Air Force affectionately dubbed the aerial cluster bombs it dropped on Finland: "Molotov bread baskets."

What Goes Up Must Blow Up

While "Bouncing Betty" may sound like the kind of high-spirited lass soldiers far from home hanker after, the term described neither a girl nor anything else a soldier wanted to encounter during World War II. Officially known as a German S-mine (for *Schrapnellmine*, *Springmine*, or *Splittermine*), the Bouncing Betty was a so-called "bounding" antipersonnel mine that had been developed in the mid-1930s and was widely used by German forces during 1939–1945. The S-mine was a metal cylinder about five inches tall and four inches in diameter, with a steel rod protruding from the top. This was the trigger. The mine was buried with the trigger upright, so that when a soldier stepped on it, a black powder charge was detonated, blasting the mine two to four feet in the air. A time-delay fuse ignited the mine's main TNT charge a half second later, setting off an explosion at just the right height to kill or injure more than a few troops. To make the blast even more deadly, the TNT was packed along with 360 steel balls, steel rods, or jagged shrapnel. The Bouncing Betty was not only deadly and deadly efficient, it also created terror in any group of soldiers who encountered it.

Foo on Them

During World War II, Allied bomber pilots reported that strange balls of light and disk-shaped objects sometimes followed them as they flew missions over Germany and Japan. The pilots of the U.S. 415th Night Fighter Squadron called these "foo-fighters," apparently after a pun on the French word *feu* (fire) that had appeared in "Smokey Stover," a popular comic strip of the period. ("Where there's foo, there's fire" was Smokey's trademark tagline.) The name stuck throughout the U.S. Army

Above: A G.I. examines a German "Bouncing Betty" antipersonnel mine he apparently just dug up—note the "skull crusher" Mark I trench knife inserted into the ground beside the hole. This was widely used not only as a close-combat weapon, but as a probe to locate and remove small mines.

Air Forces. Foo-fighters appeared to dance off the bombers' wingtips or kept pace with the aircraft in front and in back. Sightings were not limited to air corps pilots. Naval personnel, on board warships at sea, reported seeing foo-fighters maneuvering overhead.

Explanations for the foo-fighter phenomenon offered at the time ranged from ball lightning, to static electricity charges—the Saint Elmo's Fire long familiar to mariners—to evidence of Japanese and German secret weapons, intended either to foul the ignition systems of the bombers or (since the foo-fighters never actually committed a hostile action) merely to inspire psychological terror. After a cursory investigation, the U.S. Eighth Air Force dismissed the whole thing as "mass hallucination"; however, toward the end of the war, the U.S. Navy conducted studies on visual illusions experienced by nighttime aviators and suggested that foo-fighters might be the result of so-called "aviator's vertigo."

Perhaps because the sightings ended with the war, no further organized effort was made to explain the phenomenon; however, after the war, German and Japanese pilots revealed that they, too, had encountered foo-fighters, which *they* had believed were secret weapons of the Allies.

Poison Pill

No pulp fiction secret agent would ever be caught dead without his "suicide pill." The thing is, no matter how pulpy the fiction in question, the "suicide pill"—more formally called an L-pill ("L" as in "lethal")—was very real. Beginning in World War II, it was standard issue, both among Allied and Axis forces, for clandestine operatives working behind enemy lines. The assumption was that it was far preferable to end your own life quickly and relatively painlessly rather than to endure the consequences of capture: interrogation by torture, probably culminating in torture to the death.

During World War II, the typical L-pill was a thin glass ampoule sheathed in a tight, thin rubber sleeve and filled with potassium cyanide or other concentrated liquid cyanide preparation. When the chips were down and the situation hopeless, the secret agent would place the ampoule between his or her molars and bite down to break the glass, releasing the poison into the mouth. Administered in this fashion, the cyanide molecules quickly bonded chemically with the hemoglobin throughout the bloodstream, preventing it from transporting oxygen to the body. Within minutes—perhaps even less—brain death would ensue, followed by cardiac arrest. There was and remains no antidote.

While the cyanide-based L-pill seems like a pretty efficient instrument of self-destruction, the always progressive American intelligence community sought to improve it during the Cold War 1950s by using saxitoxin (STX), the paralytic neurotoxin found naturally in certain shellfish and the notoriously deadly puffer fish. STX is a thousand times more potent than the much-feared sarin nerve gas, so that just 0.05 milligrams scratched via a needle into a human being is quickly fatal. According to former CIA director William Colby, U-2 pilot Francis Gary Powers was issued an STX-impregnated needle concealed in a hollow silver dollar. Obviously, he chose not to use it when his spyplane was downed in Soviet air space on May 1, 1960. He was captured, publicly tried, convicted, and eventually released in a prisoner exchange.

Pennies Make Pounds, and Pounds Make Profits

The soldiers of Britain's World War II Parachute Regiment were issued bolt action Lee-Enfield rifles, Enfield or Webley revolvers (or M1911 pistols), and had available per unit more Sten submachine guns than were allocated to ordinary ground troops. They were also distinguished by a special uniform, including a rakish maroon beret and an airborne forces shoulder patch that featured the mythic Greek hero Bellerophon riding the flying horse Pegasus.

What they did *not* get was the security of a reserve parachute, considered standard-issue for U.S. jumpers to supplement their main chute, should it fail to open. The War Office deemed the cost, £60 per chute (about $242 in 1940, roughly $4,000 today), an exorbitant waste of good money.

Nuke It

One of the war-winning instruments of World War II combat technology was the cavity magnetron, a high-powered vacuum tube that streams electrons through a magnetic field for the purpose of generating powerful microwaves. This became the heart of radar systems used early in the war to detect incoming German bombers and thereby provide advance warning to British RAF interceptor aircraft and, of course, to the inhabitants of London and other target cities.

British and American scientists and engineers labored feverishly throughout the war to improve the magnetron and thereby advance radar technology. A native of Howland, Maine, Dr. Percy LeBaron Spencer worked as an engineer at the Raytheon Company looking for methods to step up magnetron production.

He was able to increase the rate from a quota of just seventeen finished tubes per day to an astounding 2,600. While standing in front of one of his running magnetrons in 1945, Spencer noticed that the chocolate bar he was hoarding in his pocket had melted. Discouraging though that might have been, Spencer was inspired. He scrounged some unpopped popcorn and put it in front of a magnetron. It popped, firing kernels all over the lab. Percy Spencer had just invented the microwave oven.

Within two years of the war's end, 1947, Raytheon was selling a commercial microwave oven—which Amana later marketed as (what else?) the "Radarange." Spencer copped a valuable patent, and he eventually retired in greater glory as a Raytheon senior VP and member of the Board of Directors.

☆ ☆ ☆

Your Father's Airplane

Designed as the primary strategic bomber of the United States Air Force—the flagship craft of General Curtis E. LeMay's Strategic Air Command (SAC), and the vehicle that was intended to deliver masses of atomic ordnance against the Soviet Union or possibly "Red" China—the B-52 Stratofortress first flew on April 15, 1952. Over the next decade, some 744 of this eight-engine behemoth were manufactured by Boeing in eight incarnations, designated B-52A through B-52H, before production stopped in 1962. As of 2012, eighty-five B-52H's are still in active service, with another nine held in reserve. That's a working life, so far, of sixty years, and the aircraft is slated to remain in service until at least 2045, when the design will turn ninety-three and the youngest of the operational planes will be eighty-three.

B-52 crews have long called their craft by the acronym BUFF, which USAF public relations officers say stands for "Big Ugly Fat Fellow," while the crews themselves swap out the unlikely final noun for "Fucker." Those who remain on the ground as one thunders overhead refer to it as the "aluminum overcast," while members of the B-52 pilot community wryly observe, "You may not be in your father's Air Force, but you are probably in your father's airplane."

Above: A co-pilot in the cockpit of a 23rd Bomb Squadron B-52H Stratofortress during a training sortie out of Minot Air Force Base, North Dakota, April 20, 2011. **Below:** A B-52 Stratofortress takes off on a mission during the Vietnam War. **Following pages:** This B-52H, photographed on the runway at Minot Air Force Base, North Dakota, on April 19, 2011, features nose art reminiscent of the propeller-driven bombers of World War II.

133

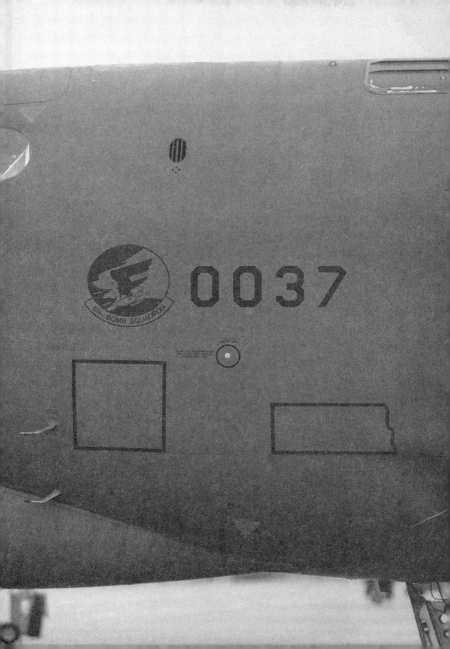

The USMC Answer to the Swiss Army Knife

In November 1942, the United States Marine Corps officially adopted the 1219C2 Combat Knife—later called the USMC Mark 2 Combat Knife or Knife, Fighting Utility. During World War II, the knife was turned out by four different manufacturers, one of which, Union Cutlery Company, trademarked it as the KA-BAR and stamped that name on it. By 1944, marines took to calling this style of knife the Ka-Bar, regardless of manufacturer.

The Ka-Bar features a seven-inch Bowie-type blade and a hilt of stacked leather washers with a "peened" pommel capable of being used as a hammer. The Ka-Bar blade is wide enough to serve as an entrenching tool and tough enough to open ration cans. Sharpened up, it can shave a face baby smooth. The grip and pommel can be used to pound tent stakes and to drive nails. In addition, the Ka-Bar kills— quickly, silently, and certainly. It is issued to marines to this very day.

People's Fighter

By 1944, Germany was on the ropes, its armies melting away on every front, its cities being pounded to rubble under remorseless air raids, its Luftwaffe (air force) reduced to a shadow of its former formidable self. Adolf Hitler desperately hoped to turn defeat into victory by deploying any number of what he called "wonder weapons." Among these was the Heinkel He 162 Salamander, popularly known as the "Volksjäger": the People's Fighter.

There are at least four remarkable things you just have to say about this airplane. First, it was tiny, with a wingspan of less than twenty-four feet, a length under thirty feet, and a fully loaded weight of no more than 6,000 pounds. Second, it was a *jet* aircraft—a type of plane the Germans were pioneering in World War II, when the rest of the world's aircraft were powered by pistons and propellers. Third, the Salamander's single jet engine was mounted on the top of its fuselage, which, like its wings and tail assembly, was made entirely of wood. That's right. The People's Fighter, top speed 522 miles per hour, was *a jet plane made out of wood*.

The fourth thing is this. The aircraft was ordered on September 8, 1944; design drawings were ready on October 30 of that very year; a prototype flew on December 6; and the aircraft was delivered beginning in January 1945. The Salamander went from idea to combat reality in a little under four months. By the time Germany surrendered in May 1945, 300 Salamanders had been delivered and were flying. Eight hundred more were on the assembly lines.

Below: This captured Heinkel He 162 was photographed on a French airfield, after the war, on September 5, 1945.

It Came From Hollywood

The United States Air Force is the youngest of the U.S. military service branches, having become independent from the U.S. Army in 1947. It was not until eight years later, in 1955, that the air force got its own academy—intended to be on par with the army's West Point and the navy's Annapolis—which graduated its first class of officers in 1959. Secretary of the Air Force Harold Talbott wanted to give his cadets a look that was distinctive from both the West Point cadet and the midshipman of Annapolis. He sought designs from all the standard military tailors, but nothing they proposed struck his fancy. That's when he called on the man who made a Moses out of Charlton Heston in *The Ten Commandments*. In 1954, Talbott asked Cecil B. DeMille—the quintessential Hollywood director (producer, screenwriter, editor, and actor as well)—to design something special for the U.S. Air Force Academy. The parade uniform he came up with had a brilliant sky-blue cutaway tailcoat with a high choke collar and a double row of silver buttons, rather like an old-fashioned bellhop's uniform. Trousers were starchy white, and a primrose-colored cavalry-style sash completed the ensemble. Talbott loved it. The generals loved it. Everybody loved it. And the U.S. Air Force Academy cadets still wear it today. Lights, Action, Afterburners!

Opposite: The U.S. Air Force Academy Class of 2011 marches into Falcon Stadium during commencement ceremonies, May 25, 2011, in Colorado Springs, Colorado—uniforms courtesy of Cecil B. DeMille.

Chapter Five

Home Front Facts

THE NOTIONS
OF BELLIGERENT
NATIONS

From Home to Graveyard

The quarter-million graves of Arlington National Cemetery fan out from the hilltop mansion known as Arlington House. This most hallowed of military graveyards, perhaps the most celebrated in the world, originally came into existence as a home and an 1,100-acre grand estate. The man who acquired the land and built the mansion, beginning in 1802, was George Washington Parke Custis. He never meant to create a cemetery, though he did intend the house and its land to serve as a living memorial to his adoptive grandfather, George Washington, who had died just three years earlier at nearby Mount Vernon.

Completed in 1818, Arlington House, which Custis was originally going to call Mount Washington, was home to Custis and his wife until they died, she in 1853, he in 1857. They became the first to be buried on the grounds. Robert E. Lee, who had married the Custises' only child, Mary Anna Randolph Custis, came to live at Arlington House when his wife inherited it. The couple and their children would occupy it only until Virginia seceded from the Union in 1861. When that happened, federal troops under Brigadier General Irvin McDowell set up positions in and around the estate, erecting Fort Whipple (now Fort Myer) and, later, Fort McPherson (now Section 11 of the cemetery). Even as the war raged, the government confiscated the estate because of Mrs. Lee's failure to pay—in person, as the law stipulated—the taxes due. Put up for sale on January 11, 1864, it was purchased by a local tax commissioner for "government use, for war, military, charitable and educational purposes." In June of that year, Brigadier General Montgomery C.

Opposite: Union major general Samuel P. Heintzelman (in front of column, center) poses with his staff on the portico of Arlington House, May 1863.

Meigs, commanding the Federal garrison at Arlington House, appropriated the grounds of the estate for development as a military cemetery.

Meigs made no secret of his intentions in claiming the property. He wanted to block Lee, the premier general of the Confederacy, and his family from ever attempting to retake the property or to live on it again. It was, in fact, a unique act of memorial vengeance.

Meigs immediately built a stone and masonry burial vault in the Lees' rose garden, in which were deposited the remains of 1,800 Union casualties. Meigs, his wife, his father, and his son were all destined to be buried within a hundred yards of the house years after the Civil War ended. In the meantime, the federal government claimed a part of the ground to be set aside as a model community for freed slaves called Freedman's Village. More than 1,100 former slaves lived there during the war.

The Lees never even attempted a return to Arlington House. Nevertheless, after Robert E. Lee died in 1870, his eldest son, Custis Lee, brought suit against the government, claiming that the land had been illegally confiscated. In December 1882, the U.S. Supreme Court, in a 5–4 decision, ordered the property restored to Custis Lee on the grounds that it had been confiscated without due process. Within months, on March 3, 1883, Congress purchased the property from Lee for $150,000, and it became what Meigs had intended it to be: a military reservation to be used as a cemetery. Although Freedman's Village was dismantled, the graves of former slaves buried on its grounds were—and remain—undisturbed.

Opposite: General Montgomery C. Meigs, commanding the Federal garrison at Arlington House, appropriated the grounds of the estate for development as a military cemetery.

What's the Point?

On March 9, 1906, Congress authorized furnishing headstones for the graves of Confederate soldiers buried in national cemeteries as well as in Confederate burial plots. Congress specified that the headstones be fashioned in the same size and of the same material as those of Union soldiers and of U.S. soldiers who had died in the Spanish-American War. There was to be one difference, however. Whereas U.S. headstones were rounded at the top, the Confederate design was pointed. Immediately, a story was circulated that one of the Confederate veterans consulted on the design of the headstones declared, "We don't want any damn Yankees sitting on our tombstones." The story stuck and is still widely offered up as the explanation for the difference between Yankee and Rebel military headstones. There is, however, no evidence that the tale is true. More likely, it was just deemed appropriate to make some simple distinction between Union and Confederate graves. A change in shape was a way to do this without necessitating the use of different materials.

☆ ☆ ☆

Cuppa Joe

The makers of Martinson Coffee—which used to call itself Martinson's Coffee—claim that when coffee drinkers refer to their beverage of choice as a "cup of Joe" (more like "cuppa Joe"), they pay homage to Joe Martinson, who came to New York City toward the end of the nineteenth century, began selling coffee from a push-cart, and grew his firm from there. The company even trademarks the phrase "Cup of Joe" and uses "It's the real Joe" as a tag line.

Not everyone agrees with this etymology, however. Some folklorists believe "joe" is short for *java*, a common colloquialism for "coffee," or for *jamoke*, a far less familiar term for it. Then there are those who say that the "Joe" is an allusion to the "Old Black Joe" who is the "singer" in the 1860 song by Stephen Foster. "Old Black Joe" is a cup of strong *black* coffee.

A more likely origin of the phrase than any of these stabs at etymology is the following episode from U.S. naval history. On June 1, 1914, President Woodrow Wilson's teetotaler secretary of the navy, Josephus Daniels, issued General Order 99 by which he abolished the so-called "officer's wine mess" aboard ship and, in fact, prohibited "the use or introduction for drinking purposes of alcoholic liquors on board any naval vessel, or within any navy yard or station." This made the United States Navy a 100 percent dry service and, in the process, elevated the status of coffee to that of the strongest drink legally available on any U.S. naval vessel. Since Josephus—"Joe"—Daniels had made it so, officers and sailors alike learned to settle for, and even enjoy, their "cup of *Joe*."

Below: In 1890, long before Secretary of the Navy Josephus Daniels decreed the service dry, the crew of the battleship USS *Massachusetts* enjoys a ration of brew.

O, Tannenbaum

Thirty to thirty-five million "real" (that is, natural) Christmas trees are sold annually in the United States, grown on some 2.5 million acres by about 20,000 growers, making it at least a $1.75 billion industry. Little wonder, since the Christmas tree is, with the Thanksgiving turkey and the Easter egg, the nation's most beloved seasonal commodity and tradition.

And we have the military to thank for it—just not the United States military.

When George Washington and some 2,400 Continentals attacked the 1,500-man Hessian encampment at Trenton, New Jersey, on December 26, 1776, they found the officers hung over from overindulgence in Christmas schnapps— and they also found Christmas trees: the very first erected in America. Notorious for their gratuitous cruelty in combat, the Hessians were troops from Hesse and other German states, pressed into service by their mercenary princes who made deals with the British government. About 30,000 served in all thirteen colonies during the American Revolution and were more earnestly hated by the Patriots than the British Redcoats who employed them. Nevertheless, some 5,000 remained in the new United States after the Revolution, bringing with them the tradition of the Tannenbaum: the Christmas tree.

The Babel Proclamation

An overwhelming majority of Americans approved of staying out of the "Great War"—later known as World War I but originally called the "European War" by most citizens of the United States. But, in April 1917, when President Wilson

Above: *Capture of the Hessians at Trenton, December 26, 1776,* John Trumbull (c. early 1800s).

sought and obtained from Congress a declaration of war, America was suddenly transformed into a nation of hawks.

Highly intolerant hawks. Just about anyone living in the United States who spoke a foreign tongue, whatever it was, fell under suspicion. In some parts of the nation, especially in the Midwest, state laws, proclamations, decrees, and local ordinances were enacted to curb or prohibit the use of German and other foreign languages in public, whether in spoken, written, or published form. In many places, German-language courses were summarily stricken from school curricula, and the U.S. Treasury Department fielded suggestions from many Americans that any bank containing the phrase "German-American" in its name should be compelled to rename itself or be shuttered. All across the United States, *sauerkraut* was instantly renamed "liberty cabbage" (much as, in 2003, anti-Gallic sentiment compelled some to dub French fries *freedom fries* early in Operation Iraqi Freedom). Even the *German measles* became "liberty measles" and *dachshunds* "liberty hounds." In St. Louis, which had a large German population, the city fathers responded to a newspaper editor's demand for "wiping out everything German in this city" by renaming *Berlin Avenue* Pershing Avenue, *Bismarck Street* Fourth Street, and *Kaiser Street* Gresham.

The federal Espionage Act and Trading-with-the-Enemy Act gave the government authority to require all foreign-language newspapers to operate under license, the licenses to be issued only after the applicant paper had been thoroughly vetted.

Nowhere was language subject to more sweeping regulation than in Iowa, whose governor, William L. Harding, issued the so-called "Babel Proclamation" on May 23, 1918, which summarily outlawed the public use of *all* foreign languages. The proclamation was the culmination of a statewide movement that had begun on November 23, 1917, when the Iowa State Council of Defense resolved that the teaching of German in public schools would be discontinued. Immediately, all German-language instructors on the state payroll were fired, and all German textbooks burned. The renaming of Iowa towns and streets proceeded apace. *Berlin Township* became Hughes Township; Muscatine's *Bismarck Street* became Bond Street; *Hanover Avenue*, Liberty Avenue; the village of *Germania* in Kossuth County was rechristened Lakota. As for the Babel Proclamation, Harding announced that it would have the full force and effect of law, and he dismissed protests that it blatantly violated the First Amendment to the U.S. Constitution. "The official language of the United States and the State of Iowa is the English language," he wrote. "Freedom of speech is guaranteed by federal and state constitutions, but this is not a guarantee of the right to use a language other than the language of this country—the English language." English—which the governor often called "American"—was to be the only language of instruction in public as well as private schools; moreover, all conversation in public places, on public conveyances, and over the telephone was required to be conducted in English. (Most arrests under the Babel Proclamation resulted from telephone operators eavesdropping on party-line conversations and reporting to the authorities those conducted in a foreign language.) English and English only was to be spoken in churches (the proclamation was silent on the subject of Latin in the Catholic liturgy and made no mention at all of worship in synagogues), and those who could not speak or understand English were required to confine their worship to the privacy of their homes.

Three on a Match

In 1919, the year after World War I ended, a new superstition swept the United States like a fad. Known as "three on a match," it held that if three people lit their cigarettes from the same match, one of them would have bad luck and maybe even drop dead, sooner if not later.

It was universally believed at the time that "three on a match" came directly from wartime trench life, where it was less a superstition than a hard fact of life in a combat zone. Light your cigarette at night, and an enemy sniper would probably see the flame—but it would go out before he could draw a bead and fire. If a second

soldier used the same match to light his cigarette, the sniper had enough time to take aim—but not to fire. Extend the process to a *third* soldier, however, and there was ample time to aim and fire. Bottom line? Someone was getting killed.

When the superstition was first bandied about in 1919, there were some who said they had actually heard their parents talk about "three on a match" from the days of the Crimean War of 1852–1856. Folklorists, however, have never been able to document an actual contemporary reference to "three on a match" during *either* World War I or the Crimean War, and some debunkers have suggested that the

Below: Yanks take instruction from a French officer at the front lines during World War I.

superstition was deliberately fabricated not in 1919 but in the early 1920s by a Swedish match manufacturer named Ivar Kreuger, who was looking for a way to frighten consumers into using and therefore buying more matches. Others have alluded to a Russian Orthodox funeral ritual in which a single taper is used to light the three candles on the altar, claiming that if you unconsciously emulate this practice in lighting three cigarettes on a single match, you unknowingly invite the occasion for a funeral.

Blitzed

The German World War II air raids on London and other British cities killed between 40,000 and 43,000 civilians, nearly half of them in London alone. Uncounted among these victims of Nazi aerial ordnance were some forty luckless pedestrians who were struck and killed by cars, their headlights deliberately masked to mere slits, attempting to navigate blacked-out city streets in the dead of night.

Opposite: Firefighters battle a London blaze the morning after a nighttime German air raid.

Chapter Six

War Records

STIMULATING STATISTICS YOU NEVER KNEW YOU WANTED TO KNOW

Oh. . .Crap!

The Thirty Years' War spanned 1618–1648, pitted most of Europe's Protestants against most of Europe's Catholics, involved nineteen countries, more than a million soldiers, and cost between eight and ten million lives, military and civilian, representing a quarter of the population of central Europe.

How did it start?

On May 23, 1618, a group of Protestants, really ticked off about having been barred from building Protestant churches in Catholic Bohemia, bribed their way into Prague's Hradcany Castle, where top Catholic councilors were meeting. The Protestants seized three of the Catholic dignitaries and unceremoniously threw them out of a third-floor window. The fall of sixty-nine feet should have killed the men, but it didn't. They were saved by a very large heap of horse manure.

Called the "Defenestration of Prague" (Who knew the English language had a one-word synonym for throwing people out of a window?), this fit of outrage ending in a pile of crap launched three decades of Europe's deadliest war up to that time.

The Long and the Short of It

The longest war on record was the "Three Hundred and Thirty Five Years War" (such is its official name) between the Isles of Scilly (an archipelago off the southwestern coast of Cornwall) and the Republic of the Seven United Netherlands. It began on

Opposite: The "Defenestration of Prague" in progress, May 23, 1618.

161

March 30, 1651, and ended on April 17, 1986. No shots were fired by either side. Not ever. No one was wounded. No one was killed.

More deadly was history's shortest war. The Anglo-Zanzibar War began at 9:02 (local time) on the morning of August 27, 1896, and ended the same morning at 9:40, by which time 500 sailors of the Zanzibar Sultanate had been killed or wounded in the sinking of two boats and one royal yacht. The British casualty count was one man wounded.

20 Percent Deadlier Than We Thought

For well over a century, Civil War historians and Civil War buffs alike have memorized two grim figures from that war: 360,222 and 258,000. These were (for many, still are) the accepted estimates of Union and Confederate troops killed, respectively. In 2011, however, J. David Hacker, a demographic historian from SUNY Binghamton, questioned, reran, and revised the numbers.

It seems that the original calculations had been the work of just two men, William F. Fox and Thomas Leonard Livermore, both veterans of the Union army and both dedicated, albeit self-trained, historians. In 1889 Fox compiled the compendious *Regimental Losses in the American Civil War, 1861–1865*. He possessed good, solid stats for the Union, but had to rely almost purely on guesswork for the Confederacy and concluded that roughly 94,000 men in gray had died. Eleven years later, Livermore took another stab at the numbers, made an even more complete count, and came up with a much larger butcher's bill for the South: 258,000 instead of 94,000. How did he do it? It turns out that, like Fox, he guessed—but he guessed differently. He decided to assume that the Confederates lost the same proportion of men to disease as the Union had lost. Having made that assumption, the numbers went up. End of story.

Below: Company F, 114th Pennsylvania Infantry Regiment, at Petersburg, Virginia, August 1864. Note their exotic Zouave uniforms. A year earlier, at Gettysburg, the 114th lost nine killed, 86 wounded, and 60 missing out of 312 men in combat.

Hacker took an entirely different approach. He compared the number of males, aged twenty to thirty, in the 1860 U.S. Census with the number aged thirty to forty, in the 1870 Census and reasonably concluded that the difference between the two figures was the number of males who died. Then he adjusted for the influx of immigrants, many of whom fought in the Civil War, especially in the Union army, and he threw out the assumption that Confederates died of disease at the same rate as Union soldiers. Medical care in the Confederate army, he knew, was far inferior to that in the Union army (which was nevertheless pretty miserable). Hacker next went beyond these revisions, also gathering figures from the 1850s and making use of newly available nineteenth-

century demographic data compiled by the Minnesota Population Center of the University of Minnesota. Crunching and re-crunching the entirety of his data, he arrived at a combined war-related death toll possibly as high as 851,066 but probably closer to 750,000, 20 percent greater than the 618,222 Civil War fatalities long accepted as fact.

Above: Medical treatment for Confederate wounded was far inferior to what Union soldiers received.
Following pages: This photograph of a Union field hospital at Savage's Station, Virginia, following the Battle of Gaines's Mill (June 27, 1862), shows just how primitive treatment for the wounded was during the Civil War.

My, That's a Big One

Schwerer Gustav—"Heavy Gustav"—and his identically proportioned sister, Dora, were the two biggest guns ever actually used in combat. Designed in 1934 and manufactured in 1941 by the fabled (or infamous) arms manufacturer Krupp, the guns weighed 1,330 tons each; had a total length of 155 feet, 2 inches; a barrel length of 106 feet, 8 inches; a width of 23 feet, 4 inches; and stood 38 feet, 1 inch high. The two guns hurled a thirty-one-inch-diameter shell weighing 15,650 pounds a distance of 51,000 yards. Transported by special railway cars, each gun required three days of assembly before firing. A crew of 250 men was required to assemble, aim, load, fire, defend, and tend the gun.

Krupp was planning to build even bigger siblings for Gustav and Dora, one that would fire 33.5-inch shells and one designed to loft a thirty-nine-inch projectile, but the war ended before these were put into production.

Safe at Home in the Third Reich

Germany was a chief aggressor in two twentieth-century world wars, which cost a combined total of some 92,043,368 human lives. Nevertheless, the pre–World War II annual murder rate in Nazi Germany was 0.75 murders per 100,000 versus 5.84 per 100,000 in the United States during this same period. The Nazi murder rate was just 12.8 percent of the U.S. rate. (America is doing a *bit* better these days, the murder rate having gone down to 4.8 per 100,000, according to 2010 stats. As of 2007, Germany was at 0.9 homicides per 100,000 people. These days, both nations are doing a lot better than Honduras, which clocked in at 78 murders per 100,000 in 2010—the highest homicide rate currently recorded among nations.)

Above: In this head-on view, the monster gun known as Heavy Gustav is shown mounted on its special railway car, which spanned two sets of custom-made tracks.

To the Last Drop

To each nation that fought in World War II, its sacrifice seemed the greatest. The United States suffered 405,399 military deaths. This terrible toll, however, did not even put the nation in the top two. China lost 3,800,000 military personnel and 16,200,000 civilians. The Soviet Union lost at least 10,700,000 military personnel and 11,400,000 civilians. When Stalin pledged to resist the Nazi invasion of the USSR "to the last drop of Russian blood," he clearly meant what he said.

Below: Red Army troops in action, Russian Front, 1942. The mounds of earth from behind which some of the soldiers fire were not intended to provide protective cover, but merely to brace their weapons.

Like Father, Like Son

General Douglas MacArthur was not so much *proud* to receive the Medal of Honor as he was *relieved*. For his many (sometimes quite reckless) demonstrations of valor in World War I, he had received a number of distinguished decorations. But the top prize, the Medal of Honor, which his father, Arthur MacArthur, had won for heroism at Missionary Ridge in the Battle of Gettysburg during the Civil War, eluded him. Douglas MacArthur believed that he had let his father down, even as he felt overshadowed by him.

At last, while he was in Australia, to which he had been evacuated during the Japanese invasion of the Philippines beginning December 8, 1941, the younger MacArthur was awarded the Medal of Honor "for conspicuous leadership in preparing the Philippine Islands to resist conquest, for gallantry and intrepidity above

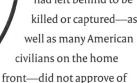

and beyond the call of duty in action against invading Japanese forces, and for the heroic conduct of defensive and offensive operations on the Bataan Peninsula." Many service personnel under his command, whom he had left behind to be killed or captured—as well as many American civilians on the home front—did not approve of

Above: General Douglas MacArthur (right) is pictured with his second-in-command, Major (later Lieutenant) General Jonathan Wainwright, in the Philippines, sometime before the Japanese assault that began on December 8, 1941. President Franklin Roosevelt's order to evacuate besieged Bataan saved MacArthur from capture, whereas Wainwright spent most of the war with his men in hellish Japanese captivity.
Opposite: Arthur MacArthur, father of Douglas MacArthur, was awarded the Medal of Honor for his heroism in action at Missionary Ridge during the Civil War's Battle of Gettysburg.

the award, even though MacArthur had been ordered by his commander in chief, President Franklin D. Roosevelt, to leave the Philippines because he was too valuable to the war effort.

For his part, when he accepted the Medal of Honor, MacArthur declared that he was accepting it as "intended not so much for me personally [but] as...a recognition of the indomitable courage of the gallant army which it was my honor to command."

The MacArthurs were the only father and son ever to receive the Medal of Honor—until Theodore Roosevelt was awarded it posthumously in 2001 for his service in the 1898 Spanish-American War. His son, Brigadier General Theodore Roosevelt Jr., had received it in 1944 for his personal leadership on Utah Beach during the D-Day landings—the only general officer to accompany his men in the first wave of the assault. Unfortunately, Roosevelt suffered from severe arthritis, the legacy of World War I battle injuries, and severe heart trouble. He died, in Europe, of a heart attack on July 12, 1944, little more than a month after D-Day, and the Medal of Honor was therefore conferred posthumously, on September 28, 1944.

Above: United States Army version of the Medal of Honor. **Opposite:** Brigadier General Theodore Roosevelt Jr. stands in front of the door to his command post in Normandy, France. Some U.S. senior officers carried canes in imitation of British commanders. Afflicted with severe arthritis (the result of poorly healed wounds received during World War I), Roosevelt needed his cane to help him walk.

Most Military Funerals Attended

Records aren't really kept for this, but it is unlikely that any human being played a leading role at more military funerals than the four-legged Black Jack.

Named in honor of General John J. ("Black Jack") Pershing, commander in charge of the American Expeditionary Force (AEF) in World War I, Black Jack was a sable-black Morgan-American Quarter Horse cross. He was assigned to the Caisson Platoon of the Third U.S. Infantry Regiment, the unit known as The Old Guard, which officiates at many ceremonies in Washington, D.C., with none more important than military funerals. Black Jack appeared in more than 1,000 Armed Forces Full Honors Funerals (AFFHF) as the saddled but riderless horse, boots reversed in the stirrups, symbolizing the fallen warrior. He became something of a national celebrity as the spirited steed that was led in the televised funeral procession of President John F. Kennedy (1963), and he also participated in funerals for Presidents Herbert Hoover (1964) and Lyndon B. Johnson (1973), as well as for General of the Army Douglas MacArthur (1964).

Black Jack had been foaled on January 19, 1947, and began his service at Fort Myer with the Old Guard on November 22, 1952. He was the last of the Quartermaster-issue horses branded with the Army's "U.S." brand and issued an army serial number, 2V56. His own death came on February 6, 1976, after twenty-nine years of military service. Cremated, his ashes were interred in a plot at Fort Myer, Virginia, with Full Military Honors.

Opposite: The funeral procession for President John F. Kennedy, November 25, 1963. Black Jack, without a rider, is led behind the caisson that bears the slain president's casket.

The Last Soldier

Hiroo Onodo (1922–), a Japanese Imperial Army intelligence officer, was assigned to Lubang Island in the Philippines on December 26, 1944. As he sent him to his new post, Major Yoshimi Taniguchi, Onodo's commanding officer, ordered him never to surrender—and never to commit suicide.

Hiroo Onodo took his orders very seriously.

While Lubang fell to U.S. and Philippine forces on February 28, 1945, Onoda and three other soldiers hid out. Months later, they found air-dropped leaflets announcing the end of the war, but discounted them as Allied propaganda and disinformation. When more leaflets were dropped, bearing General Tomoyuki Yamashita's signed surrender orders, Onoda and the others agreed that these, too, were tricks.

In 1949, four years after the war in the Pacific ended, one of the three men under Onoda's command walked out of hiding, wandered the jungle for six months, and then surrendered to Filipino forces in 1950. Two years later, Filipino aircraft dropped letters and family pictures on the area in which Onoda and his remaining men were known to be holed up. It was hoped that these documents would convince them to surrender. They did not.

Left: Young Hiroo Onodo, Japanese Imperial Army.

In 1953 and 1954, there were shootouts with locals—the second encounter resulting in the death of another of Onoda's men. Then, on October 19, 1972, the last of Onoda's troops was shot and killed by local police. Finally, on February 20, 1974, Norio Suzuki, a young Japanese man self-described as a college dropout, who claimed that he was tramping across the world in search of "Lieutenant Onoda, a panda, and the Abominable Snowman, in that order," succeeded in doing what nobody else had. He not only found Onoda, he talked with him.

Although Suzuki soon won the lieutenant's confidence—and even his friendship—Onoda, though acknowledging an end to the war, nevertheless insisted on waiting for official orders from a superior officer. Accordingly, Suzuki returned to Japan, presented government officials with photographs of himself with Onoda, explained what Onoda wanted, and persuaded the officials to locate the lieutenant's World War II commanding officer, Yoshimi Taniguchi. Although he was now the comfortable owner of a bookstore, Taniguchi did not hesitate to fly out to Lubang. He met Onoda on March 9, 1974, and handed him his personal order:

> In accordance with the Imperial command, the Fourteenth Area Army has ceased all combat activity.
>
> In accordance with military Headquarters Command No. A-2003, the Special Squadron of Staff's Headquarters is relieved of all military duties.
>
> Units and individuals under the command of Special Squadron are to cease military activities and operations immediately and place themselves under the command of the nearest superior officer. When no officer can be found, they

are to communicate with the American or Philippine forces
and follow their directives.

Officially and formally relieved of duty, Onoda was not required to surrender. As for the shootouts, Philippine president Ferdinand Marcos personally issued an executive pardon, and the former lieutenant returned to Japan, where, as of this writing, he still lives.

Opposite: Old Hiroo Onoda, Japanese Imperial Army, relieved of duty on March 9, 1974. Note the white handle of his Samurai sword.

About the Author

Alan Axelrod is the author of more than 100 books on history, military history, and leadership.

After receiving his Ph.D. in English (specializing in early American literature and culture) from the University of Iowa in 1979, Axelrod taught early American literature and culture at Lake Forest College (Lake Forest, Illinois) and at Furman University (Greenville, South Carolina) before entering scholarly and commercial publishing. In 1997, he founded The Ian Samuel Group, Inc., a consulting, creative services, editing, and book-packaging firm in Atlanta.

Axelrod has been a featured speaker at the Conference on Excellence in Government (Washington, D.C.), at the Leadership Institute of Columbia College (Columbia, South Carolina), and at the Annual Conference of the Goizueta School of Business, Emory University (Atlanta). He has been a creative consultant (and on-camera personality) for *The Wild West* television documentary series and A&E's *Civil War Journal* and has appeared on the Discovery Channel, MSNBC, CNN, CNNfn, CNBC, Fox Network affiliates in Philadelphia and Atlanta, and numerous radio news and talk programs, including National Public Radio. He and his work have been featured in *BusinessWeek, Fortune, Men's Health, Cosmopolitan, Inc., Atlanta Business Chronicle, Publishers Weekly*, and many newspapers, including the *Atlanta Journal-Constitution, Boston Globe, New York Times*, and *USA Today*. He lives with his wife, Anita, an artist, in Atlanta and in the Blue Ridge Mountains of western North Carolina.

Image Credits

© **akg-images** — 103

© **Associated Press** — 45, 108

Army Heritage & Education Center, Carlisle PA — 63, 119

Art Resource, NY — © Heinrich Hoffmann/Bayerische Staatsbibliothek/bpk: 169

Bridgeman Art Library — 110-111

Corbis — © Hulton-Deutsch Collection: 31; © Bettmann: 43, 64, 170-171, 175, 176; © Michael Nicholson: 73

Depositphotos — © Panos Karapanagiotis: 48

Department of Defense — Cpl Mondo Lescaud/USMC: 46-47; PH2 D. Wujcik: 68-69; 127

Courtesy of www.doctormacro.com — 42

Courtesy Dover Publications — 1, 10, 71 inset, 76, 80-81, 164-165

Dreamstime.com — © Susan Mcannally: 146

Everett Collection — 58; © CSU Archives: 178

Courtesy of D.M. Giangreco — 122

Harper's Weekly, 1864 — 85

The Image Works — © ullstein bild: 27

iStockphoto — 160

Library of Congress — 12-13, 13 inset, 15, 18, 25, 28, 36, 47 inset, 51, 55, 56, 61, 75, 77, 78-79, 87, 88, 91, 100-101, 107, 115, 117, 121, 123, 124, 140-141, 141 inset, 143, 145, 148-149, 151, 154-155, 158-159, 162-163, 166-167, 173

Courtesy James C. Nannos — 108-109

National Archives — 29 left, 40, 70-71, 95, 96-97, 101 inset, 118, 132-133, 137, 157

Private Collection — 53, 62, 159 inset, 172

Naval History and Heritage Command — 34-35, 35 top

US Air Force — Staff Sgt Andy M Kin: 133 top, SSgt Jennifer L Flores: 134-135, Bill Evan: 139

US Army — 29

US Marine Corps — Quantico Base Library, VA: 39

Courtesy West Point Museum Collection, United States Military Academy — 57, 59, 174